TO AL...

The Gift of Adversity

YOU'RE only
AS STRONG AS
THE ADVERSITY
YOU overcome!

Table of Contents

The Gift of Adversity

"Out of suffering have emerged the strongest of souls."

-Khalil Gibran

This book is dedicated to all whom find themselves in the midst of Adversity.

-Marcus Aurelius Anderson

Chapter I

Sweet Dreams

"You're never more alive than when you're almost dead."

-Tim O'Brien-

Deadline.

The word sounds rather ominous as if someone's drawn a line in the sand and once you cross it, you're no longer alive.

Thursday 04:30

My alarm is going off. I roll out of my warm bed and sleepily look out the window. It's snowing, again. It hasn't stopped snowing from the previous day and night. During the winter months at Ft. Drum in upstate New York, it was always snowing. Located roughly 30 miles south of the Canadian border and coupled with the lake effect from nearby Lake Ontario, precipitation was a constant year-round. I put on my long thermal underwear and socks as I checked the temperature. It says its -5 degrees outside, but the wind chill factor says it feels like -20; a perfect day for a ruck march in the 10th Mountain Light Infantry division.

This morning we are going to stretch our legs with a 10-mile, 50% ruck march. The "50%" signifies the amount of your own bodyweight that you pack into your rucksack. I still smile when I think of the irony of such a name, "Light" Infantry. The rucksack I was going to be carrying today alone was 90 lbs. Then add to that our full Battle Rattle of 50 lbs. of plate body armor, a Kevlar helmet, my M4 carbine, and three quarts of water that inevitably froze during the march. The ice and snow made the load we were to bear for the next 10 miles feel even heavier. There was little that we ever carried that was light, to say the least.

"Light" Infantry my ass.

The crowning jewel of our combat ensemble was our gas masks designed for combat in chemical environments. These were employed on our march to create artificial oxygen deprivation simulating conditions in the mountains of Afghanistan. Though it may sound extreme, these are the methods that are required to prepare us for war in the Korengal Valley.

These marches began at a standard ruck marching pace. This can be anywhere from 12 to 15 minutes per mile depending on the snow and ice, but every platoon in our company was incredibly competitive so these marches would always end up turning into more of a jogging pace as each platoon would push ever harder to try to outdo the other.

Originally a Light Infantry unit specializing in mountain warfare in arctic conditions, 10th Mountain was activated to battle the Nazi's in the Mountains of Italy during World War II. 10th Mountain's illustrious military history includes deployments in Operation Desert Storm, Operation Enduring Freedom, and Operation Iraqi Freedom; as well as other peacekeeping deployments. 10th Mountain is known for being featured in the book "Blackhawk Down," which was later made into a movie chronicling The Battle of Mogadishu in 1993.

With our inevitable deployment approaching, this meant the already intense training was taken up a few notches.

The entire week had been full of our standard PT (Physical Training): long distance running, ruck marches, rope climbing, repelling, combatives/hand to hand combat training, obstacle courses, weight training, and our tactics and weapons training. Fitting in any specialized training, equipment, and weapons maintenance—and the week gets full rather quickly. We had just returned from a week in the field so they wanted to keep us busy, but a crazy week of hard training was the norm, and a relief, compared to the previous week spent in the field.

In the Army I had reinvented myself, joining at the ripe old age of 38. My Great Uncle had been a huge role model for me when I was a boy. He served in Special Forces during his multiple tours in the Vietnam War. I'd always wanted to serve my country as he had and after my divorce, I realized my window to get into the military was closing quickly. I had no wife or children to hold me back; I was out of excuses and now was my time to act.

The recruiter had to sign a waiver to allow me to join as the age limit at that time was 35, but I did well on the PT test, and my written test scores were off the charts. He saw that I was very motivated to join, so he signed the waiver. He was not too pleased when I told him about the MOS I'd chosen. He kept telling me, "Listen, Anderson, your test scores, and PT scores are outstanding! You can literally do ANYTHING you want in the Army, and you want to go Infantry? Seriously!?" I explained to him my desire to follow in my Uncle's footsteps. He begrudgingly told me, "hey man it's your life," as we signed the pertinent paperwork.

I got in excellent shape before I shipped out to basic training. Having the ship date was a very real deadline, and knowing that I would be asking more from my mind and body that I had possibly in my entire life created the motivation needed to be as physically prepared as possible.

Of course, I still had plenty of trepidation as I entered basic training and Infantry School at Ft. Benning, Georgia.

Would I be able to make it through? Would I get injured and not be able to complete the course? Could the training be worse than I thought it would be in my mind? How would I do compared to the younger guys there? Would I be the oldest recruit? (Yes, I was actually older than many of the Drill Sergeants.) In my mind, I was envisioning my basic training would be like the movie "Full Metal Jacket" and prepared myself for such hardship. Luckily, my age and maturity level made my mind even stronger than my body, which gave me an advantage. I was in the best physical and mental condition I'd ever been in my life. This preparation allowed me to push my body beyond all preconceived boundaries, going far beyond what I thought was even possible.

After March

Friday 05:30

I woke up the morning after the 50% ruck very slowly. It was as if my body wouldn't obey my mind's commands. I attribute this as simply soreness and stiffness from the last few weeks of training. I chuckle and silently scold myself for my weakness, making a mental note to do extra heavy squats and deadlifts this weekend to remedy this problem. My body finally responds, and I'm able to get out of bed and start to get dressed.

I stand up but have to put my hands out to catch myself on the wall to stand. Damn, my balance is off too. That was going to make PT a little rough this morning, but I'll survive. Luckily, we were doing much lighter PT this morning than we had been. Just a 3-mile run, some rope climbs, push-ups, pull-ups, and sit-ups. It would only last for about an hour; then we'd be released to get some chow.

It was cold again this morning, not as cold as yesterday, but still cold none the less. My feet and hands were already numb while I was standing outside in formation. As we begin our run, my legs just wouldn't go. I couldn't even feel

4

the ground under my feet as we started running. I was able to keep up, but it was much harder than it should've been at this easy pace. Push-ups and sit-ups were okay, but for the life of me, I couldn't hold onto the rope or the pull-up bar. My hands felt like they had huge, thick pillows on them. I've always had good grip strength, so this was a bit concerning as well. Maybe I should just take the weekend to rest instead of adding heavy squats and deadlifts as previously thought.

After PT I take a hot shower and feel a little better, though my hands and feet are still numb. I look carefully for signs of frostbite as I shower, but find no such indicators. I put on my ACU's and sit down to put on clean socks and boots. I can hardly feel the socks with my hands, and my feet feel as if they are asleep from lack of circulation. What should take a minute turns into a 15-minute ordeal while my boots end up looking like an intoxicated 3-year-old tied them. It takes so long that I have to forgo breakfast to ensure that I get to formation in time. It's a good thing I did because my walking pace was much slower than normal, having to swing my legs heavily one in front of the other like a couple of overfilled sacks of potatoes.

The rest of the day was not physically demanding at all, filled with safety briefs, meetings, and paperwork. We were able to leave by 17:00 and have a weekend off which was a novelty for the Infantry. Everyone else was planning on going to get some dinner and drinks later that evening, but all I wanted to do was get back to my place so I could relax and recover. I knew I just needed some rest and my hands and feet would be back to normal the next morning.

Saturday 06:00

A noise outside my front door wakes me up. I attempt to turn my head to look at the clock, but I can't seem to move my head and neck. I try again, this time with more vigor. Still nothing. What the hell? I attempt to log-roll my entire body onto my left side, but my body remains unmoved. My entire body from the neck down feels numb and unresponsive.

As a child, I remembered nightmares of being chased by something that paralyzed me with fear. In these dreams, I couldn't move or even see what was chasing me. Lying in my bunk, I realized that this was my worst nightmare come to life.

I am unable to move, and I am beyond terrified...

Chapter II

Scrubs

"I learned that every mortal will taste death. But only some will taste life."

-Rumi-

I'm rushed 80 miles south of Ft. Drum by ambulance to the hospital in Syracuse, New York. As I'm being wheeled into the hospital on a gurney, there's a whirlwind of activity around me and I'm swarmed by people who are talking loudly about me as if I'm not there.

A cardiologist is running a scan of my heart while a neurologist is poking and prodding me, looking for signs of neurological deficiencies. Other doctors and nurses are briskly walking while shining pen lights in my eyes and rattling off my vitals as I can only lie there and watch from my supine point of view; just like a scene from a movie. I'm sure it would look exhilarating and impressive to behold this scene as a bystander with all the bells and whistles, but from where I lay, it's becoming abundantly apparent that I'm more seriously injured than I previously believed.

I've had my fair share of bumps, bruises, and stitches in my life, but I'd never been injured seriously enough to require admittance to a hospital before. The small army of doctors and nurses giving this kind of attention all at once is starting to concern me. I mean, is all this attention necessary? Maybe they are just overreacting. I've still got things to do, I have priorities, and I don't have time to be hurt. My platoon is deploying soon, and I've got to be ready. Walking quickly next to me with his hand on the gurney is Corporal Buddy Jacobucci. I can tell by the serious look on his lean jawline that this display by the medical staff has him concerned as well. Having someone I trusted and respected next to me to help endure this hardship is all I could ask for in my current circumstance.

I'm wheeled into a room and hooked up to an I.V. and a bunch of other machines that monitor my vitals and who knows what else. At this point, I start to feel an incredible pain at the base of my neck. It's getting worse with each breath I take, and my breathing is becoming labored. Jacobucci goes and quickly finds a nurse to tell her about my symptoms. She says she'll be back soon. I hope that she does because the pain continues to worsen, it feels like my head is about to explode. The nurse returns with a doctor who looks at my vitals, then they both leave again. Jacobucci has seen enough incompetence demonstrated, so he goes and finds the nearest nurse and tells her in a civil but stern tone "this soldier is in tremendous pain, isn't there something you can do for him?" She comes back moments later with morphine. She puts it into my I.V., and I can barely thank her before it sends me to Nirvana.

Still flying from the morphine, I don't remember being transported to the MRI bay, but the thunderous tumbling of the MRI machine certainly gets my attention. It reminds me of grenades and machine gun fire. A voice over the speaker tells me to stay still, which clearly isn't a problem in my present condition. The scan is over before I realize and they whisk me back to the room I was held in previously. Jacobucci's waiting there for me. "How you feeling man?" he asks. "The morphine is still there, but it's starting to wear off a bit," I reply. Another nurse comes in and says "OK, time to get you prepped." Corporal Jacobucci takes the words right out of my mouth, "Prepped for what exactly?" The nurse looks confused by the question as she looks at the both of us, "Well, for surgery of course." Hearing her statement must have caused the rest of the morphine in my bloodstream to evaporate instantaneously because now I'm as sober as a hangover.

Surgery

As I'm being wheeled down to surgery, my mind is trampled with questions. What the hell is wrong with me? Does it really require surgery? Will I ever be able to walk or use my hands again? Am I going to be like this for the rest of my life? What if something goes wrong in surgery? When we get down to the hall outside the operating room, there is a team of 8 people there. "Are you all here because of me?" I ask. My question gets a collective laugh, which doesn't really put me at ease. "Well damn, how bad off am I? If it requires all of you to be here then it can't be good." That's when each person introduces themselves, telling me the part they will be playing in my operation. Many of the people there are a back-up to the primary person in my surgery. The anesthesiologist has a person there to take over in case something happens to him during the operation. The other people there have back-ups and overlaps too. While this is reassuring, it almost makes me more nervous. If they need this many people to make sure I don't die during surgery, then they must have a big job ahead of them.

The neurologist goes on to explain my MRI findings. It turns out my C5 disc in my neck ruptured, or as he put it "looks like it exploded on the MRI. I've never seen one that bad before!" Wow, lucky me. You never want to be the patient that is so messed up that doctors are calling in other doctors to say, "Hey come here, you've just got to see this!" The disc has ruptured completely and is pressing into my spinal column, essentially choking my spinal cord. The pressure is so great that it isn't allowing any cerebral spinal fluid (CFS) to flow down below the C5 disc level. The surgery will be a discectomy to remove what's left of the disc which will hopefully relieve the pressure on my spinal cord. They will also do a fusion of the C5 and C6 vertebrae to stabilize my neck. They will go in with a titanium plate and screws through the front of my neck to fuse the two bones permanently. The metal will stay in my neck for the rest of my life, a little memento of my experience. Evidently, all the intense military training had caused more wear and tear on my body than I'd realized. It seemed the cumulative effect of attrition was more debilitating than I thought. As I'm being told this, I'm still nervous, but now I'm somewhat hopeful. I ask "So, that means I'll be back to normal again? I'll walk and be able to use my hands like before, right? I mean, that's what you're telling me, correct?"

Silence.

Silence is never a good answer, especially when it's such an important question. One of the doctors tells me that hopefully, that's the case. "Hopefully? What do you mean hopefully?" I'm becoming even more nervous because of this non-committal answer. Can't someone just give me a straight answer? He goes on to explain that there is damage to my spinal cord from the degree of compression and impingement, so there is a possibility of some long-term effects. "What the hell does THAT mean?!" I say as I start to raise my voice. I'm no longer nervous; now I'm just getting angry. "What kind of long-term effects? Would being like this for the rest of my life be considered a "long-term effect" from this injury!?" I say as my voice grows louder. The entire group is now trying to calm me down. One of them tells me to try not to worry about that right now, just to try to relax and stay calm. Get through the surgery first, then worry about recovery and rehab. While this is a logical argument, it's hard to think this way when I'm the one who's about to go under the knife. At this point, they tell Corporal Jacobucci he has to leave so I can go to the operating room. He looks at me and says, "Hey man, don't worry. See you on the other side." He pats my shoulder reassuringly as he leaves.

As they wheel me into the operating room, one of the nurses tells me that she and the team are going to take extra good care of me because I'm a soldier. That because I've been injured while trying to prepare to defend my country that I'm a hero, and that they take extra good care of heroes. While this sounds good and probably even makes her feel better by saying it, I don't agree with her. I simply say, "thank you" and lie on the table trying to calm my nerves, realizing that it's all out of my hands at this point.

I consider the soldiers who have and are currently deployed to be heroes. I think of police, fireman and first responders as heroes. I'm just a guy who was trying to prepare to defend my country as best I could. And now here I am in a hospital, about to have a major operation because of it. Man, how the hell did I end up here? This train of thought is derailed as they put the anesthesia mask over my face. I realize now that there's literally nothing else I can do other than try to remain calm and hope for the best.I feel like I'm slowly cresting at the top of the highest roller coaster known to man, unable to see what lies beneath me. The nurse tells me to start counting down from 100 as the anesthesia begins to flow. I get to 97 and...

**

It's very dark. I feel nothing but cold and see only blackness.

**

Hospital ICU

My eyes slowly open and I'm in a room I don't recognize. Where am I? What day is it? Wait, am I supposed to be in formation right now? Am I AWOL?! People are poking and prodding me again, looking at the displays on the machines I'm hooked up to. I try to speak, but my throat feels as raw as a blue steak, and no words come out. A nurse makes eye

11

contact with me and smiles. "Well, Mr. Anderson you're back among the living." I try to reply but she shushes me. "Don't try to move your neck; we have you in a brace. We also have you on a catheter, so you don't have to worry about having to use the bathroom. Don't try talking for a little while; I'm sure your throat is sore."

I must still be in a mild state of shock. I try to process this barrage of information, but can't. I lump this new information in with the growing stack of the other chaotic information I've received, but still haven't processed over the last 24 hours. As the nurse is leaving she says, "Just get some sleep Mr. Anderson, you've been through a lot. People will be back and forth checking on, you so you might as well just try to get some rest."

I'm in and out of sleep for the next few hours. Right when I'm asleep, I'm woken by a different person entering my room, which continues for the rest of the afternoon until I see a familiar face enter. My surgeon comes in and grabs a chair. He has a seat at the foot of my bed in front of me, sitting down within my line of sight. "How are you feeling?" he inquires. "Your throat probably hurts so don't worry about responding." Being unable to speak or nod my head, I just listened as he continued. He clears this throat a few times before he begins to speak. "Well I'm not going to lie, you had us worried there for a little while," he said laughing a little nervously as I lay in bed still unable to move from the neck down. Worried? I was the one getting cut on; I thought I was who was supposed to be worried during the surgery. "The surgery ended up lasting longer than expected. It took us over six hours to get it done. You crashed hard on us; I didn't know if we were going to get you back there for a minute. That happened a few times actually."

Crashed? What did he mean crashed? Didn't know if they were going to be able to get me back, back from where?! Evidently, the look on my face expressed every question I was thinking but was unable to verbalize. "Hey, consider yourself lucky Mr. Anderson, you died and lived to tell the tale. Twice!" I must have heard him incorrectly. Did he just say I'd died?! His sentiment had a congratulatory tone to it. I was speechless, but this time it wasn't because my throat was raw from the tubes that had been desperately crammed down my throat to save my life during the operation. I was beside myself. I couldn't believe it. Was this whole experience just a crazy dream? Am I going to wake up in my bed at Ft. Drum and realize that none of this ever happened?

My surgeon proceeds to tell me more about the surgery. I can see his mouth moving, and his facial expressions seem positive and reassuring, but I can't hear a word he's saying. The only thing I can hear are the words still echoing in my head from before. The words that told me I'd died. Literally flatlined. TWICE. That was my last thought as I drifted back to sleep. The staff in the ICU took great care of me during my recovery. One nurse in particular, who worked the night shift, always made sure I had everything I needed. She even went out and got me my favorite ice cream to help soothe my raw throat. The following night during her rounds, we struck up a conversation. Well sort of, I'd try to talk, and she'd try to listen and answer my questions.

The next morning, I had another visitor. Corporal Jacobucci was in the chair when I woke up. He gives me a wry smile, "Hey man. Glad you're finally awake, I've been waiting forever. Is sleeping the only thing you do here you lazy ass?" These are the first words I hear this morning. Classy. What a way to start the day. I smile back just as wryly and give my raspy, single word answer, "Yep." The familiar, sarcastic busting of my chops is a welcome relief to what I've been dealing with recently. It's nice to have a laugh and break the tension of the situation a bit. "So when are you getting the hell out of here?" I think Jacobucci wanted me out of here as much as I did. "The nurse says it'll be a few days at least, and then they will decide from there," I slowly replied. "Good man, the sooner we can get you out of here, the better...because you look like hammered dog shit," he says with a smile. Yes, Jacobucci always knew the right thing to say to make you feel good in any situation.

Before I can respond in kind, a couple of nurses enter the room to check on me. One of them asks about my pain levels. I realize that my neck doesn't hurt too badly, but that I still can't feel anything from the neck down. She explains that there is still some powerful pain medication in my system from the surgery and that it should be wearing off soon. Jacobucci informs me he has to get back to Ft. Drum. "I'll tell everyone there that you're not dead. I'll be down again to check you out of the hospital when the time comes...if you're not still sleeping of course."

The Question

That evening the nurse who got me ice cream returned, and we were able to have an actual conversation. We had developed a bit of rapport now that I had somewhat regained my voice. As our discussion continued, she asked if I'd gotten to talk to my surgeon about what happened during my operation. I replied that I had, and as we were talking she wanted to know if she could ask me a personal question. I could tell she was a little reluctant, but I obliged.

She said, "I don't mean to sound morbid or nosey," she paused. "Yes?" I said, "Go on?" She was quiet for a moment then continued. "I know this is going to sound weird, so I'll just come out and ask, and remember you don't have to answer if you don't want to." "I said it was fine, what's your question?" She sat still looking away from me, then she finally looked down at the floor and asked, "Did you see anything when you were, you know....?" Sensing her hesitation and wanting to ease her discomfort, I replied, "When I was, what? You mean when I was dead?" I gave a disarming smile, showing I gave her permission to agree to her request. She saw my expression and finally said, "Yes, when you were...dead." There it was. It sounded strange hearing those words spoken out loud. It was like this entire ordeal had been a bad dream, but the act of verbalizing it suddenly made me admit that it was a reality. The question hung in the air as I processed its gravity.

To be honest, I hadn't thought about it. The previous 72 hours had been a blur, and I was always in some state of transport, examination, operation prep, or recovery; none of which gave me a moment to even consider what the next few days would hold for me, let alone the huge question of mortality. I furrowed my brow and thought hard. I tried to remember, what did I see? Did I see anything? I mean, I must've seen something, right? My mind raced as it was suddenly flooded by every story I'd heard about people having near death or out of body experiences. Stories of people who had stepped across to the other side for a brief moment and time stood still for them. Frozen in this eternity, they always came back with some enlightened jewel of knowledge, wisdom beyond this world. I must have taken a lot of time contemplating this, because eventually she cleared her throat and said, "I'm sorry, I didn't mean to make you uncomfortable."

Something in her voice snapped me from my trance and primed my memory of the event. I DID remember seeing something now. YES! Slowly I began to remember; it was coming back! I HAD seen something! Yes, it was a bit hazy, but gradually it became incredibly clear. The more I concentrated on it, the more I saw it there right before me. It was colossal, magnificent, and all-encompassing. My eyes recognized as it finally came into focus. What I saw I'll never be able to forget because of its impactful significance. I saw...

Darkness.

Nothing.

Zip.

Zilch.

Nada.

I didn't see anything. Nope. Sorry folks. I could lie and tell some incredible story about an out of body experience or an awe-inspiring vision that told me the secrets of life on this mortal coil, but I'd rather disappoint you with the truth than impress you momentarily with a fable.

To clarify, when other people tell stories about the things they saw after a near-death experience or even death, I have no reason not to believe them. Even after my own experience, I take them at their word. I believe that they genuinely saw and experienced something. There is all kinds of research that discuss the release of chemicals that rush into the brain when a person dies. Whether their vision was a neurological inducement from Dimethyltryptamine (DMT) or a person seeing God in Heaven surrounded by glorious angels is up for debate.

Perhaps I was on too powerful of anesthesia to see these things. Maybe their biochemistry was just different than mine, at least in that moment of time. Regardless, I have the utmost respect for people who saw something that was of significance to them, which reinforces or perhaps even brings them back to a faith or belief system that they may have lost sight of.

There are all kinds of religious and philosophical discussions, explanations, and debates that could be lobbed from all sides to justify why someone did or did not see what they saw. Many believe that if a person has a vision while they are in this state that it was a lesson they needed to learn or be reminded of. Each person's belief regarding God, the Universe, and the afterlife is uniquely their own, and I have the highest respect for that. All I can tell you for certain is what I experienced during my unique circumstance. I'll let you the reader interpret this however you see fit. Take it for what it is. It's death, and death is a fact of life.

Chapter III

War of Heart

*"Most of us have two lives. The life we live, and the
unlived life within us."*

-Steven Pressfield-

My 40th Birthday

A 40th birthday is quite a milestone. It is the birthday seen
as the marker of a person's achievements. A time of
reflection. Many people at this point in their lives have
things pretty much figured out.

They have a job where they've been employed for a number
of years. More than likely married with a family, a
mortgage, two cars, and a pet or two. They can take it a little
easier now and don't have to work quite as hard as when
they were first starting out. At least that's the expectation I
had growing up, but life happens on its own terms and
timeline, and there is never a perfect time for anything,
ever.

Here's the reality: in this life, there are basically three
things that can happen. What we hope will happen, what
we fear will happen, and then what actually happens.

My 40th birthday was a huge milestone for me as well, but it was nothing like what I mentioned. I'd been in the Army for only a couple of years, and now it was apparent that I'd never deploy. Call me crazy, but I was still hoping that there was a way I'd be able to recover and serve my country through deployment.

(The irony is that later that same year President Obama came to Ft. Drum to announce to the United States that he was "bringing the troops home." He was making good on one of his original election promises, which just so happened to occur while he was running for his second term. This meant that 10th Mountain was not going to be deploying anytime in the near future. Needless to say, I didn't have anything figured out. Not by a longshot.)

I turned 40 years old broke, divorced, bedridden, and wondering if I'd ever be able to walk or use my hands again.

Let that statement sink in for a moment. My whole world had been turned upside down. In an instant, I went from preparing for war on the battlefield to a war within my own body and mind. I remembered reading stories and seeing movies about people who'd been seriously injured and disabled. While these stories were compelling, I still lived my life up to that point like others who had that 'oh it won't happen to ME' attitude.

The realization of my injury was sobering. I felt like a statistic. The harsh reality that slapped me in the face was that I was ashamed of how I'd wasted my life up to that point, at least that's how it felt when faced with the possibility of being bedridden for the rest of my life. I had wasted so much time, talent, and potential thinking I'd always have the time, talent, and potential to do whatever I wanted to do.

The more I thought about it, the madder I became. I was beyond angry; I was positively furious with myself for being so lazy and short-sighted! I remembered all the times I'd asked lesser of myself because I thought, "well, there's always tomorrow, I'll just do it then." And for what? To put off my future so that I could sit my ass on the couch and watch the newest episode of whatever TV show was hot at the time?! So, I could catch a nap?!

Rehab

After months of convalescence back at Ft. Drum to recover from my surgery, I was cleared to begin physical therapy. When I was going through my rehabilitation and doing all kinds of physical and occupational therapy, I must admit that my outlook wasn't always exactly "positive."

There were days when I didn't want to go to at all because frankly, it didn't seem to be working. It was as if the rehabilitation was pointless. But there was more to it.

Honestly, I was embarrassed. I didn't want people to see me struggle and continually fail. I went from feeling the highest of highs- like an indestructible superhuman of a soldier- to the lowest I'd ever been in my life after my injury. Being unable to do something as simple as walk or hold a water bottle without dropping it made me feel like I was useless. I was completely demoralized by my injury.

One Step Forward

Then one day, I got some good news. After a few weeks of physical and occupational rehabilitation, I was finally able to move my feet! It wasn't much, but it was at least something! I felt I'd turned a corner. I was beyond ecstatic! I was finally making some progress! The idea that I could get my life back now seemed within my reach. Even after this good fortune, trying to learn to walk again still seemed almost impossible at times. Instead of getting easier, it seemed like it was getting more difficult by the day.

In the rehab facility, there was a three-stair tall staircase that was used to help soldiers learn to walk again. Just three steps, that's all. Trying to get my numb legs to climb even a single stair was a daunting task. Climbing all three would be out of the question for a long while. Struggling with something that I would normally be able to do without a second thought with such difficulty was an arduous endeavor.

Suicide

Then the bad news. Unfortunately, a week after my breakthrough, I plateaued and found no improvement. My physical therapist said that this wasn't uncommon to have a little relapse and to just be patient.

Not long after, my condition worsened, and I regressed. Within another week I was nearly back to where I was when I first started physical therapy. To say that this was a soul-crushing development would be an understatement. Being given a glimmer of hope only to have it snuffed out so quickly was almost more than I could handle. I wanted to give up. I was tired of trying in vain and felt almost completely defeated.

After losing what little movement and feeling I'd been able to regain, I went into a deep depression. I tried to stay positive, but I don't care who you are, no one can stay continually positive when they are going through the hardest event of their life.

As time passed without improvement, my depression grew deeper. These were my darkest days, and if I'm honest, I can tell you that there were times when I thought I'd rather die than live the rest of my life in my current state. I was growing desperate.

After being painfully honest with myself and even wrestling with the thought of taking my own life, I began to understand something. I now knew why people took suicide into consideration, and it may not be for the reasons you believe.

I came to understand that people who really think about suicide don't necessarily want to kill themselves, at least not initially. It's just that they see no other choice, no reason worthy of enduring this hardship called life. They want to live, and they have desperately searched for a reason to live, a purpose. They look for purpose everywhere outside of themselves but find little. When they have looked over and over, time and again throughout their lives for something deserving of this level of devotion, they were always disappointed and left wanting. Sadly, if they don't find purpose they believe that suicide is the only option.

Wasting Potential

But here's the dirty little secret; the secret that I knew to be true, but I never wanted to admit to myself. The secret was this: even before I enlisted in the Army and got injured, I knew deep down that I wasn't doing what I wanted to do, that I was wasting my potential. I found myself doing what those around me seemed to be doing, just going with the flow, doing just enough to get by.

I had nothing to give me a sense of urgency. I'd been living my life like I was waiting for something. I was sitting back and expecting amazing things to just 'happen' to me, thinking that greatness would just knock on my door out of the blue as if I'd won the lottery.

I realized that greatness doesn't happen by accident. I had became so complacent in life because I believed it would take a Herculean effort on my part to reach even a small amount of greatness. I'd have to be willing to make many sacrifices to get where I wanted to go.

Of course, the irony of this is that by comparison to the hellish turmoil I was going through with my injury, my previous idea of Herculean effort wasn't even a drop in the bucket compared to my current circumstance.

Like everyone around me, I lacked purpose. I looked externally to find it but found that to be ultimately insubstantial and unfulfilling. I kept hoping that I'd one day see a sign that told me what to do, what my destiny was. I was never courageous enough to ask myself a few difficult but simple questions to give me direction.

What did I want?

What did I believe in?

What was truly important to me?

What was my purpose?

Laying in a bed paralyzed, I felt guilty for not accomplishing more with my life, as if my injury was the Universe's way of punishing me for wasting all the potential I'd been given but never bothered to actualize.

Need for Purpose

Without purpose, we lack direction. Without direction, our lives simply meander down the path of least resistance. We become controlled by a purely reactionary or strictly pleasure-seeking existence. We are constantly putting out fires and in some ways waiting to be victimized by things we are unable to control.

Having a purely reactionary mindset creates an existence that makes you feel like you have no control of your life and are constantly one step behind. Being caught up in this kind of cycle does not allow the opportunity or concentration needed to find the things we are lacking, or the ability to recognize that we lack in certain areas in the first place.

This can leave us susceptible to boredom, which causes us to seek distraction to fill the void. These distractions can range anywhere from simple and relatively harmless preoccupations to more dangerous or even life-threatening personal abuses. We seek distraction because we still possess as a species a vague residual instinct that tells us we are unfulfilled and unsatisfied. Therefore, we are continually searching for something, but like a person who rambles on and on while telling a story and then forgets the point they were trying to make, we get caught up in the multitude of mild distractions that keep us preoccupied for the moment.

We then become overwhelmed and give into mental and emotional fatigue, causing us to steer towards the most easily reached destination- any port in the storm as it were. We again put these important decisions of purpose and direction on hold "until tomorrow."

These moments of temporary distraction become the norm, and sadly, a way of life. Each moment piles onto the other, the days pass, and we search in vain for something we can never quite put our finger on. Inadvertently, instead of searching to find purpose, because we are too far removed from the sight of that truth to recognize it's a necessity, we now seek the next bigger, better distraction to keep us more heavily occupied.

Unfortunately, many confuse comfort and distraction with success and satisfaction. Nothing could be further from the truth.

"Misery loves company, but not as much as mediocrity."

-Marcus Aurelius Anderson-

Giving up your dreams and ambitions doesn't happen overnight. It happens in slow, easily digestible increments. We let our current situation dictate our next, which is often either out of fear or our perception that we lack other options.

Giving up on your dreams and ambitions doesn't happen overnight, but still, it happens regardless. It happens one compromised decision after another. Of course, we justify these decisions to ourselves. It's in our nature to tell ourselves that we'll change. The human mind can justify anything. Remember, even a serial killer justifies his actions.

We Settle

We settle for the job we don't want, but we take "for now." We then become accustomed to the routine, repetition, salary, and lifestyle it provides.

We tell ourselves that we will keep looking for a better job while we work our current job. After a week or two, we abandon that idea, though it doesn't feel like we've given up on this notion completely. We just think that we'll give ourselves some time to settle into this new job and THEN we'll start looking for the job we REALLY want.

This temporary job for many becomes permanent. And while we are aware of this possibility, we refuse to admit or acknowledge it because it is uncomfortable to do so. We settle for the relationships we have "for now."

Consequently, the people we meet and interact with during these times are often in the same situation. They are of a similar mindset and therefore appear to have the same ideals and interests as you do. This is because you are both programmed by the same stylized distractions that have kept you (pre)occupied this entire time.

It is this familiarity that is often mistaken for preference and therefore, happiness. They watch the same TV shows, consume the same social media, like the same sports and belong to the same ideologies that you do. So, naturally, these are the people you associate with, and, by default, prefer.

This holds true of romantic relationships as well. Though initially enthusiastic, the relationship quickly becomes subdued, because the relationship is looked upon by both parties, like everything else in their lives, as a form of entertainment and distraction. While the couple isn't entirely happy, they are too lazy or fearful to break it off and find someone more stimulating.

After some time has passed in the relationship, someone in the couple comes up with the bright idea of moving in together so they can both save money. This makes sense to both because they've already decided previously to settle for the job that they took "for now" which, of course, doesn't pay as much as they'd like to create financial independence in the first place.

These less than ideal relationships can skew our minds and emotions into thinking that what we feel for this person is love. This can lead to a marriage out of boredom, loneliness, or desperation due to fear and insecurities. These insecurities can feed into or create a co-dependent mindset. We've lowered our standards and expectations already in so many other facets of our lives, so why should this come as a surprise to you? We settle for our body "for now." We grow too undisciplined to change our eating, activity, and workout habits because we value these distractions and routines that we are now so accustomed to more than we do the possibility of being, looking, and feeling healthier.

We have replaced our hunger for knowledge and adventure with the hunger for our favorite beverage and foods filled with the experience of empty calories and little to no nutritional value that they provide.

We settle for our mind and mentality "for now." Instead of taking time to be mentally present, meditate, pray, or even read a book, we let ourselves coast through a day-to-day existence.

We mindlessly consume social media with an ADD-like focus looking for the newest distraction. We let media outlets from all sides of the aisle wash over us, telling us what we should think, feel, love, hate, and purchase. These things usually just so happen to fall in line with their political or advertising agenda in some capacity, both of which creates profits for them.

We settle, over and over again, in every aspect of our lives, and what is tolerated, is what will continue. The gravity of the situation isn't fully felt or understood oftentimes until it's too late, again by our own choosing. In other words, we settle for our boring, uninspired lives. We allow the mundaneness of this pattern of existence to define us from day to day, thought by thought, and interaction by interaction.

We have no one to blame. We can't blame our genetics, our parents, our upbringing, our teachers, or school systems. We can only blame ourselves, because we chose this, remember? It all stemmed from the decision of inaction. The simple choice of choosing not to choose, of intellectual procrastination. This is the very definition of anxiety. The first domino to fall creating this result was our lack of purpose, our lack of discipline, and inability to ask ourselves the few important questions needed to find what we believe. By allowing procrastination to become the norm, we never get around to answering these questions.

The irony is we didn't want to pay the small price of becoming momentarily uncomfortable, to be honest with ourselves. By doing so, we ended up paying a far greater price, in the long run, wasting a tremendous amount of time being swept from situation to situation. The Lesson? Don't settle. Period.

All Hope is Lost

After I regressed back to square one of my recovery, I'd given up all hope. I can say with all honesty that I did not want to go on. I felt defeated and wanted to stop trying. I'd lost the battle. I was in a downward spiral of depression, and somehow I knew I was approaching the bottom. Innately, I also knew that death is what awaited me there.

The knowledge that on average 22 veterans commit suicide every day kept running through my mind. I even began to contemplate ways to take my own life. I could almost smell and taste its presence. For a brief moment, I let this defeat hover over me. Even in the face of this Adversity, I knew the truth. I realized that if I was somehow able to take my life now, that I'd be settling too. That if I gave up, it would mean I would be settling for what my life had been up to this point. I had no idea what my future held for me, but after this unflinching self-inspection I knew one thing to be certain; I wasn't about to sit on my ass and play a victim for the rest of my life. At that moment, I came to terms with what was relevant and what was not.

Battles are not relevant, wars are, and I'll be damned if I was going to lose this war.

Fear

Eventually, I found something else that drove me. Something that was not positive or nurturing, but incredibly motivating none the less. The thing that drove me is an emotion we all possess. My motivation? Good, old-fashioned fear. Fear can take many shapes and forms. It can be paralyzing and stop you dead in your tracks, arresting your movement and decision making.

Fear can make you run around like a wounded gazelle in every direction as it burns through you like wildfire. It can manifest as boredom when a person is overwhelmed by a daunting task, and of course, one of the most commonly misconstrued faces of fear is procrastination. This active form of avoidance lets the person momentarily put off the inevitable discomfort and pain of the task that demands their attention, the situation they fear.

I was more afraid than I've ever been in my entire existence. I had been through many hardships and tribulations in my life up to this point. Even during those times when I wasn't sure about my future, I still had faith in myself and my abilities to get me through, but now I was terrified and desperate.

All these things that I'd always taken for granted changed in the blink of an eye. It was the fear of losing these things that had been ripped from me that caused my fearful desperation. Moreover, I now feared I'd never be able to even live independently again. The thought of needing a nurse or caregiver for the rest of my days was an even more demeaning possibility.

Dawning

When you are completely enveloped by darkness, you are able to see the light with ease. It was at this lowest point of my deepest depression, when I was surrounded by complete darkness, that I had an epiphany. Suddenly, everything became clear.

The vision I had when I flatlined, that wasn't emptiness, and it wasn't me staring into nothing. It wasn't an ending. It was a new beginning; a blank slate. It was a place to start fresh, to begin anew. To start over but this time, with redoubled efforts and more importantly, a burning purpose. My experience had given me new insight and perspective into my life and what I now needed to accomplish with it.

Bitch Slap

Life has a way of jolting you out of your daze and getting your attention. Sometimes it must shake you violently and say, "HEY! I'm trying to get your attention! Wake up, look at your life! Is this what you want? Is this what you REALLY WANT?!" My death and paralysis was the bitch slap from life that I needed to help open my eyes and snap me out of the slumber of mediocrity. It took my death to make me truly begin to LIVE.

The following chapters are a representation of what I've learned from my experience. I present them as actionable lessons and stories to offer you the ability to create a personal plan of action. With proper preparation, commitment and mindset the templet you create can be life-changing when coupled with the discipline of execution.

My passion is to help you find purpose. To help you understand that you have so much underutilized potential and that the time to use these abilities is fading away faster than you may realize. It's not too late to make it happen, but you must act on it now while you still have the energy, enthusiasm, and time to bring it to fruition. My goal is to teach you to create the mentality that gives you the courage and resolve to attack and overcome your personal Adversities, whatever they may be. Armed with this knowledge, you will commit to your goals and purpose with reinvigorated effort to reach success.

The reality is that with every moment that ticks by, you drift further from your goals and ambitions. If any of this strikes a chord in you, it's because you realize as I did, that eventually at some point you'll be too far removed from these things to be able to act on them.

That is why you must begin as soon as possible. Think of my story as a vicarious life-changing event for you. Learn from my hardships and channel that knowledge into action. Allow the lessons I learned from overcoming my Gift of Adversity to inspire you and set your ambitions in motion. I learned these lessons the hard way, paying an enormous price for this wisdom. By acting on this knowledge and truth now without having to go through the pain and hardship I have will save you time, energy, and possibly your life.

This book was written specifically for you. This is your wakeup call from the slumber of mediocrity. This is your kick in the ass to get up and start living your life and achieving your goals NOW.

It took losing everything that I thought was important to give me a sense of urgency. This legitimate urgency is what is needed to genuinely pursue happiness. Sometimes life strips away all other options from your grasp, leaving you no other choice except to follow your dreams. It often takes something life-changing to help find purpose. You must commit completely, and you must allow yourself no other options, no contingencies.

Chapter IV

Epiphany Ever After

"When it comes to something I truly want, I will single handedly storm the gates of Heaven or Hell to get it."

-Marcus Aurelius Anderson-

After my epiphany, I committed wholeheartedly to regaining as much of my previous physical capacities as I possibly could. I was giving myself one last chance to actualize my potential in every respect. I acted as if my life depended on these efforts because, in reality, it did.

With this level of intensity in mind, I began to map out my game plan to get back that which I had lost. This plan encompassed a multi-pronged approach.

Every morning I would wake up and tell myself that I was strong beyond measure and that I could overcome anything, including this current Adversity. I would also remind myself that I was lucky just to be alive, that I was grateful for everything in my life, both good and bad. Now, before you think I'm singing the same old song that you've heard so many times before, let me elaborate further.

"Tactics without strategy is the noise before defeat."

-Sun Tzu-

You know the tune of which I speak. The one that infers that by just saying happy things and having a positive mindset, everything in your life will automatically change for the better. That by simply employing happy thoughts and having a positive attitude, you will magically get everything that you've ever wanted in your life. This ideology believes that the simple act of belief is all that is needed to achieve success, financial security, and happiness. While there is some semblance of truth to this, there is far more to it than indulging in the childlike fantasy of blissful ignorance. For every person who has thought positive things and gotten a significant change, there are just as many people who have tried it and gotten zero results. If all you do is think about success, it is no better than thinking of your favorite nursery rhyme and expecting that to become a reality. To achieve anything in this life, you must take action. The reality is that Law of Attraction only works as hard as you do.

On the other end of the spectrum, there are those who have a more "blue collar" ideal of success. They feel that all that is required to reach your goals and ambitions is a strong work ethic. People of this opinion believe that if you keep blindly moving forward, you will eventually succeed. Therefore, if a 40-hour work week isn't enough to get what they are after, no problem; they will just put in more time and work 50 hours a week. While this is admirable, it quickly becomes a self-defeating proposition. For example, if increasing your work week from 40 to 50 hours is what is required to reach your goals, then so be it. However, there are a few issues with this mentality.

The first issue is that while you may not mind working that many hours, especially if you are desperate for the money it provides, there may come a time when you aren't able to put in that amount of work. Perhaps you become sick, injured, or have a family emergency that doesn't allow for this amount of time.

Another problem arises if the job you are working slows down, which in turn can't schedule you the hours needed to reach your monetary goals. Maybe you can only be given 40 hours a week because the busy season of work has slowed down, making it impossible to make the same money you were when you were working 10 more hours a week. It doesn't work in the long term because there aren't enough work hours to do what they need to reach their goals.

Lastly, there are only so many hours in a day. Perhaps initially going from 40 to 50 hours a week moved you closer to your goal monetarily, but what happens when you realize that you need to be working closer to 60 hours a week to meet your goal? Like the first example, perhaps fear can drive you to work at this rate initially, but eventually, you will become mentally and physically exhausted and soon face burn out, putting you back where you started.

You can work hard at a dead-end job for the rest your life and never be financially successful. Even if you work harder than any of your co-workers, there are still limitations in the amount of financial compensation you can potentially gain. Working 80 hours a week at $10 an hour is a losing proposition. So, if both schools of thought are so flawed, what's the answer?

"Knowing is not enough, we must apply. Willing is not enough, we must do."

-Bruce Lee-

The answer is to create a hybrid of any and all categories specific to your goals and needs. This often overlooked missing third component of this collective approach is the creation of a plan and vision. If you do not have an accurate roadmap to your destination you can work hard while going in circles indefinitely, eventually succumbing to fatigue and ultimately failing in the process.

This more eclectic mentality recognizes the shortcomings of the previous reasoning's and improves upon them while taking the most useful aspects to create a more efficient form of thinking and application. It demonstrates that hoping and thinking positive things is good, but it's not nearly enough to succeed in your endeavors. It also points out that having a great work ethic means little when it's applied in the wrong endeavors. Hoping for something, but not following through with action, is but a fool's wish- and subconsciously, everyone knows this. No matter how perfectly created, there is no plan, in and of itself, that will do the work to achieve your goal. A million-dollar idea that isn't executed makes a net of exactly $0.

The people who talk of how belief and conviction helped them, achieved their goals by working their asses off while being committed 100% to their desired result. They applied a blue-collar work ethic in addition to their positive mindset to be successful. You must dream like an optimist while working like a pessimist. Then, and ONLY then, will your mere thoughts have positive repercussions. With all of these components in place, you can begin to create your template of success.

Finding Passion

People always talk about finding their passion, and that once they've found it, they never have to work a day in their life. However, this notion can be misleading.

The reason people can work so hard at something that they are passionate about it because it is indeed their PASSION.

For example, think of anything that you enjoy and are passionate about, anything from a new hobby you enjoy to your favorite charity. Now, think of how much harder you would work doing that passion than you would doing something else that you feel isn't worthy of your attention, effort, and time. This is the missing piece of the puzzle that people never seem to put together. They believe that they can do something that they enjoy in the same passive, casual manner that they are currently engaging in and expect to get amazing results.

This is a fallacy. Even if you are pursuing your passion, there will still be days when it feels like a grind. There will be times when it feels like it's hard work because guess what? It IS hard work! The reality is that your passion will drive you to endure more, to work harder, longer, and more efficiently than the motivation to get a paycheck doing something you are not passionate about pursuing.

To illustrate, think of an interest you have currently. It could be anything that you enjoy. Now, think of how you would feel about it if you were required to do it while punching the clock at least 40 hours a week. Would that change how you view this hobby? Take working out for example. Many people enjoy going to the gym because of all the benefits it provides. Now imagine if you owned that same gym and were required to be there for 12 hours at a time, while not working out. It would change your attitude about being there because having to clean up after other gym members, seeing the numerous mistakes in form as well hearing the same conversations over and over would soon grate on your nerves. Instead of being able to just workout and then leave, you would be dealing with the daily headaches of being a business owner, such as worrying about bills and growing your business.

The Gift

After my accident and all I'd been through, I was very thankful just to be alive. I was even more grateful to have a chance to begin again, but what I was the most thankful for may surprise you. The thing that I was most thankful for was the incredible gift my injury gave me. The Gift of Adversity.

What is The Gift of Adversity?

Adversity is a natural law. Like the Law of Gravity, it's doesn't care about your opinion when you are trying to lift something heavy. If you can't handle the burden, then too bad, that's not Adversity's problem. You see Adversity everyday whether you are aware it or not. It comes disguised as hard work. It may show itself as a huge setback that will stop every inch of progress you have made and even cause you to lose ground. It might present itself as the biggest endeavor you have ever had thrust upon you, at the absolute worst possible time with an almost impossible deadline. Undoubtedly at the time, Adversity will appear to be the worst thing to ever happen to you in your entire life.

Why is Adversity a Gift?

In Steven Pressfield's phenomenal book, "The War of Art," he speaks in depth about the force and phenomenon that he deems "Resistance." He goes on at length to describe the many ways Resistance can get in your way and block you from your goals. He tells how Resistance knows you inside and out and, therefore, knows all your weaknesses. Is can provide a compelling argument to slow down and seduce you from being able to do the very thing you are trying so hard to accomplish.

I see Adversity much in the same way Pressfield sees Resistance but to a higher degree. Adversity is a meaner and more aggressive big brother of Resistance. So why do I call Adversity a Gift? Think of Adversity as a challenge that you have no choice but to accept, an offer you can't refuse. Adversity is the trainer who sees that you want to give up during the hardest part of your workout but doesn't let you quit. It sees that you have a little more to give and it forces you to wring out every last ounce of effort you possess.

Adversity is the Drill Sergeant who is yelling in your face the moment you step off the bus at basic training. Adversity is the Martial Arts instructor who disciplines you when you act without respect, humility, and integrity.

Adversity is the parent who grounds you after you're caught trying to sneak out of the house at midnight, or perhaps catches you sneaking back in.

Like all of these examples, at the time, Adversity feels incredibly harsh and ruthless. It acts with heartless regard for what you desire at that moment. Adversity makes you drop everything you're doing to give it your full, undivided attention. Adversity shows up uninvited at the most inopportune times without apology. Adversity couldn't care less about what you want. Adversity doesn't give a damn about your feelings. Adversity doesn't take no for an answer.

Adversary

Frankly, it feels like Adversity hates you, and it does, it absolutely does hate you. It only hates a particular part of you. What part of you does it hate? The weak part.

The physical manifestation of Adversity is an Adversary. Adversity and Adversary come from the root Adverse, all stemming from the Latin adversus meaning "against, to oppose, opposite." Though it may sound counterintuitive, an Adversary is our best teacher. Nothing shines a light on your weaknesses better than someone who contests your strengths with intensity. There are many great lessons to be learned, and each of these lessons requires a new Adversary to teach us what we must learn from it.

Think about it—an Adversary is one of the most honest people you will ever encounter. They wear their hate for you openly on their sleeve. It is impossible to misconstrue their intent, and even though they want to do you harm, at least they are honest about it. That is more than can be said about some so-called friends. Adversity, like an Adversary, forces you to question your resolve. It presses you to say, "I don't know if I can do this." In that moment of self-inquisition, feel grateful. For the question itself builds greater strength within you, and your Adversity will act as the catalyst for that to happen.

One of the greatest lessons we can learn from an Adversary is the lesson of humility. From humility, we come to understand that we learn 100X more from a loss than we do a victory. There are few things as motivating as the thirst for redemption. A loss causes us to look at our shortcomings from a raw and honest standpoint, allowing us clarity that we lack in the heat of battle.

In martial arts, there is a saying, "I either win, or I learn." For this very reason, Adversity is something we as human beings must go and actively seek out to reach a higher level in any endeavor. Without Adversity, we become stagnant and complacent. You must seek the Adversity that you most wish to overcome. Trying to become mentally and emotionally strong without encountering struggle is like trying to make your body stronger without touching a weight or working out. In the end, we are only as strong as the Adversity we overcome. The pain will eventually subside, but the lesson will always remain. If you look hard enough, you find that experience will strengthen you to endure the next battle. Only this time you will be stronger and wiser than before. Pain and discomfort are always the best teachers. Adversity is the gift that teaches and strengthens us, causing us to reach far beyond where we ever thought possible.

It's About Choice

You must make up your mind and make the conscientious choice to strive for greatness, and you must keep making that choice, again and again. Every. Single. Day.

Why? Adversity will ask you every single day if you want to quit. It will offer you the opportunity to just give up at any moment. It will throw distraction, temptation, and boredom at you to keep you from moving forward even an inch.

Adversity forces you to focus on what you truly want by sacrificing other things that, while valuable, aren't as worthy of the sacrifice as your Priority.

How do you make that choice? By acting. Your actions will reveal your decision when Adversity presents itself. If you haven't acted, then you have already decided— you've decided not to do anything to change your current situation. Even if you call it procrastination, it's still a decision, a decision to do nothing.

The beauty of Adversity is that after we've passed through it, we can look back and see that it wasn't as bad as we thought it was at the time. In hindsight, we can see Adversity for what it is, something that forces us to improve and push much further than we ever imagined possible.

Without Adversity prodding us mercilessly, we'd have given up long before we reached this level.

Adversity forces you to up your game and play at a higher level. It never lets you coast or do just enough to get by.

Adversity knows when you're slacking or acting 'busy' instead of being productive.

Adversity doesn't buy your silly excuses, and it calls bullshit when you try to say the dog ate your homework.

Adversity knows your full potential, even if you do not, which is why it kicks your ass when you try to half-ass it.

Adversity knows the truth, so you can't expect to lie and get away with it.

Adversity is a gift because it doesn't allow the opportunity to cop out. It's the ultimate form of tough love, you can't escape it.

Adversity offers you no other choice, and when there's no other choice, the choice is simple. During my recovery, I realized that if I could overcome this Adversity before me, even if only mentally, I could overcome anything else Adversity had to throw at me. After I decided to see my Adversity as a gift instead of a curse, something miraculous began to happen in my life...

Moving Forward

Certain things need to be put in place for you to move forward and maximize your potential. The correct mentality to allow maximum clarification of purpose and intent is imperative when seeking this valuable knowledge.

Therefore, from this moment forward, there is something you must do. You must take full responsibility for where you are right now. You need to be brutally honest with yourself and realize that everything that you have ever encountered, every roadblock, every stroke of bad luck, every bad break that you've told yourself is holding you back, is an excuse.

Read that last sentence again.

The reality is that most people have never really had to face any true Adversity in their lives. They have had it too easy; therefore they don't appreciate the things they have at their fingertips. Without struggle, we don't truly value the things we currently possess. Without hardship, we cannot truly appreciate the luxuries we have in the palm of our hands.

The reality is that Adversity is relative. No matter the hardship you or I have endured, there are plenty of people throughout history and who are alive today who have gone through and overcome far greater Adversities than you or I have or will ever encounter.

There are literally millions of people all over the world who would give anything to have the opportunity that you are taking for granted this very moment.

Clarify

Adversity is an inevitability. It is never a question of if we are going to face it, it's a question of the degree of Adversity we will have to endure when do encounter it. We can never escape it completely. For this reason, I choose to take a philosophical approach when it comes to Adversity. Let's be honest, it's not as if Adversity it's going to just turn around and leave you alone. Even after you overcome it once, you know it's going to come back around again in some way, shape, or form in the future. By developing a thicker skin and stronger resolve, it allows you the opportunity to face Adversity again and embrace it more powerfully this time.

It is this mentality and mindset that helps us press through the next Adversity that much faster, allowing us to continue forward in our progress. None of us like Adversity at the time. Seriously, it sucks. If you do not look at it from a philosophical standpoint and just see it as a horrible hardship that you do not want to endure, then you may not get past. You'll be stuck in the exact same place that you are now unable to evolve and grow while being miserable the entire torturous time.

"The best way out is through."

-Robert Frost-

How do we defeat Adversity? By facing it, head on. If you try to escape Adversity, it can crush you. By attempting to go the long way around Adversity, you may never be able to circumvent its grasp. By trying to avoid the struggle, you not only have to face the same Adversity that you would have anyway but now you'll be forced to do it fatigued from the effort of trying to avoid it in the first place.

The very act of trying to avoid Adversity reduces your chances of success because Adversity is an inevitability in the path to succeeding. It would be like trying to avoid the tide while swimming in the ocean. Like the ocean, if you can learn to embrace the tide of Adversity, you can learn to let it lift you up, and ride the wave to shore unscathed. If you can keep your head in the moment, take a look around as you ride the wave of Adversity. The view is absolutely breathtaking.

You must learn to embrace the Adversity. You have to look at it with the attitude of "this is going to suck, but I'm going to be stronger after I get through this." It is this mentality that allows you to look at any form of Adversity with a bit of swagger, to smirk and keep moving forward.

You must believe that you can endure and overcome anything that Adversity can throw at you.

If a chain is only as strong as its weakest link, then a person is only as strong as their greatest fear and their ability to overcome it. But, let me clarify.

Do not misconstrue my desire to embrace Adversity as a reason to live a reckless existence. I'm not suggesting to intentionally get into a car accident or walk into a rough part of town and try to get into a knife fight. Moreover, I am also not implying that people who have endured heart-wrenching tragedy in their lives should be happy about it. People who have been beaten, raped, and sold into slavery; or even worse, have endured much more than what I'm referring to as Adversity. They have endured hell on earth.

The Muhammad Ali of Cambodia

In 2015, I had the honor of meeting and training with a Cambodian fighting legend. I was attending a martial arts seminar at the world-renowned Inosanto Martial Arts Academy in Marina Del Ray, California. Guro Dan Inosanto was teaching a seminar with Cambodian Boxing Master Oumry Ban.

From the late 1960's to 1975, Master Oumry Ban was a Pradal Serey Champion fighting in his home country of Cambodia. Winning 270 of his 309 Muay Thai fights, 200 of those by knock out, Ban was a known as "the Muhammad Ali of Cambodia."

(Pradal Serey means freestyle fighting in Cambodian and is the Father of Muay Boran and the now popular Muay Thai.)

During the chaos of the Vietnam War, Cambodia was consumed by civil war. In April of 1975, Cambodia suffered a hostile takeover by the Communist Khmer Rouge regime. The leader of the Khmer Rouge, Pol Pot, ruled with an iron fist. To ensure that there would be no resistance to his rule, he had an estimated 2 million people executed in the deadly "Killing Fields" of Cambodia.

Anyone who was considered a potential threat to the Khmer Rouge was killed or put into concentration camps. This included Pradal Serey practitioners because their knowledge of this devastating Martial Art was considered dangerous. Oumry Ban knew that his celebrity in Pradal Serey would make him a target.

Narrowly escaping with his life and now desperate, he lived in the mountains for over a year surviving on whatever he could scavenge and living off the land as best he could.

Oumry Ban had lost everything. His entire family had been killed in the Cambodian Genocide. He had no possessions except for the clothes on his back. He had no money or trophies from his time as a Cambodian Boxing Champion and national hero.

To this day, he has only been able to recover one surviving picture of him fighting at the height of career. Eventually, he escaped to the Philippines. When he finally made his way to the United States, he opened the Longbeach Kickboxing gym where he still trains fighters to this day.

Even while in the safety of United States, Master Ban was still unable to escape Adversity completely. In 2006 Ban was ambushed by three assailants and beaten within inches of his life.

Today, even after all this Adversity, Oumry Ban smiles. When you meet him he shakes your hand, his smile beaming. How can a man who has endured so much in his life be so happy? Because through all the Adversity of his 72 years of life, he understands. He understands what a gift it is to be alive. He knows that after all he's seen and experienced, that life is indeed a privilege.

So, as we see, Adversity truly is relative.

The fact that you are reading this means:

1. You are educated enough to read.

2. You have enough money to purchase this book and/or to have access to the internet to download it.

3. If you have money for these less essential things, then you more than likely have enough clean water to drink, food to eat, and a roof over your head.

These three things alone dictate that you are better off than more than 3/4 of the population on this planet. When you are honest with yourself, you come to realize that most of the problems you have now aren't problems, they are inconveniences. Most of what you are calling pain, is merely discomfort.

Endowed with the knowledge that you are better off than the vast majority in the world and that the things you consider obstacles are not that hard to overcome, then I ask you: why aren't you achieving more of the goals you want to achieve?

Here's why:

It's not that you lack time. People waste countless hours daily on all kinds of mindless activities from social media to Netflix. If the average American saved $12 a day (the price of coffee and a sandwich), they'd have enough money to purchase a plane ticket to anywhere in the world in 4 months.

It's not that you lack time.

It's not that you lack money.

It's that you lack genuine priorities.

Now that there are no more excuses, it's time to focus. It's time to ask yourself what it is that is truly important to you.

Chapter V

Back to Basics

*"Efforts and courage are not enough without purpose
and direction."*

-John F. Kennedy-

Deathbed

When a person is on their deathbed, many thoughts go
through their mind. They think of the people they love and
care about the most, those that they cherish. These
thoughts include their spouse, family, and beloved friends.
It's also a time of introspection to take stock of what their
life has meant to them and others. While many may believe
that's what the end of their life will be like, the fact is, we
may not have the foresight of finding out when we are going
to die due to disease or old age. In other words, we may not
be given the luxury of time for the recollection of our life
experiences. Dying suddenly with barely enough time to
have our lives flash before us is a distinct possibility.

If that is the case, when will we have this chance to take
time to reflect on what we've done with our lives up to this

point? When will we be able to consider how we feel about what we've accomplished thus far in our journey? How will we know if we are satisfied with what we've done, the direction we've gone, and if it's been a worthy investment of our time? The time to do all these things is now.

By taking the present moment to reflect, it gives us the chance to see where we've gone and allows us to consider the direction we want to go from here. It gives us the opportunity to appreciate the people in our lives and the things we've accomplished, no matter how large or small those things may be.

Your life can change in a moment as mine did, and after that moment has passed, it is impossible to go back. I acknowledge that there are those who may have a less sagacious mentality in this respect. Some may be of the opinion that if they are going to die without a chance to contemplate their existence, then what's the use in even going through the mental exercise of doing so? They don't realize the benefits to be reaped from the process.

While they are correct about the end result that awaits us all, it shows that they aren't taking into consideration their impact on others. Having this kind of selfish attitude paints them into a corner intellectually. Whether you are aware of it or not, you are making an impact on those around you just by your sheer proximity to them. A simple interaction that you may not give a second thought could mean the world in the eyes of another. Just as easily, something done that was never meant with even a hint of ill intention could have a huge negative effect.

The Purpose of Life is to Live a Life of Purpose

In the end, it comes down to one question: do you want to make an impact with the life and time you've been given, or do you just want to exist? You may be alive, but actually living while making the most of your life is the goal. When you understand that you can still live your life and do all the things you've always dreamed of while simultaneously improving the lives of others, you will have a greater understanding of what you want to accomplish in life.

If you're the kind of person who thinks that they don't have the time to take stock now and that they'll just do it later, I'll allow you that indulgence. But first, there is something you must come to understand: Later is a prolonged term used by many because it is more palatable than saying never. If you are just trying to kill time, remember that time will always win that battle.

Brutal Honesty = Ferocious Optimism

"I'm brutally honest with myself, but that allows me to be ferociously optimistic."

-Marcus Aurelius Anderson-

The mentality of a person on their deathbed is one thing, but I wasn't on my deathbed, and the mindset of an otherwise healthy person who is paralyzed is something altogether different. If you are bedridden and still have possibly another 30-40 years of your life to live, the things you think about are a little different than the person on their deathbed. Your thoughts go to the things you didn't get done and the regrets of things you wished you'd at least attempted before you were no longer able to walk. While contemplation of regrets is something a person on their deathbed will surely think about as well, the potential consequences were, in a way, more significant for me.

These thoughts become more prolific when you consider that in my current condition, I could be alive yet paralyzed for many more years to regret these things that I might still never be able to accomplish physically. I could potentially have another half lifetime of bitter disappointment and anguish that would slowly eat away at me from the inside.

From this Gift of Adversity, I have gained tremendous insight into the human condition. I've learned that the toughest parts of life aren't the hardships you are enduring currently. Whether its family responsibilities, stress from your job, or financial challenges; these aren't the most difficult elements of life.

The hardest part of life is when you are no longer able to do these things. When you don't possess the ability to continue these difficulties, you may find yourself missing the hardships that you are currently present. When you look back on your life and see things that you'd always wanted to do, things that you could have been great at if you'd only have applied yourself, and realize that there's no longer time to achieve these things, that's perhaps the most difficult part.

Is This It?

I urge you to put yourself in my position wondering "is this it, is this all the time I have?" Realizing that I indeed had so much more I wanted to get done in my life and that I had barely scratched the surface made me feel as if I was drowning within sight of the shore.

When you are lying bedridden, examining what is valuable in your life, you notice a few things. Things that are counterintuitive to what modern society believes, but you will find that they ring loud and true none the less. You will realize your education or lack thereof will mean next to nothing to you at this point. Your time in school and higher education is just a vacant memory. The size of your house, the kind of car you drive, and brand of clothes you wear will matter not. The amount of money you have in the bank will be a number on a computer screen or slip of paper. No matter how large or impressive that amount may be, it can neither buy you more time nor improve your current physical condition. If all the things that the majority of society today thinks is valuable are without much worth, then I ask you, what is important?

That's a very good question.

Questions That Matter

This is the time, your time, to reflect. This is the time to set aside a few minutes and be brutally honest with yourself. Remember, the more brutally honest you are now, the more ferociously optimistic you can be about your future. Take at least a few minutes to reflect solely on answering each question. Feel free to ponder longer if you wish or to come back after the initial allotted time. The idea is to not rush through these questions quickly. They are worthy of your time and effort.

Write down your answers here in the book or on a separate document. Write down everything that comes to mind. Do not stop writing until you start to repeat yourself, only then will you have concluded your thought process.

So here we go...

Beyond the obvious hopes of getting all your physical abilities back, of course, ask yourself the hard questions that are unique to you specifically:

If you woke up tomorrow paralyzed from the neck down, what would you wish you'd have accomplished with your life?

What do you wish you'd have done?

What lingering regret(s) would you harbor?

If by some miracle you were able to recover, how would you live your life differently than you had before?

Answers

The things that are coming to your mind RIGHT NOW this very moment, these are the things that are truly important to you. These are your actual Priorities. These are the things that mean the most to you in this time of hardship and should, therefore, mean a tremendous amount to you right now. These are the things that if given the opportunity, you'd jump at the chance to start doing and working on immediately. These are the answers that matter.

Adversity teaches many things. We can be afforded certain myths of belief around something we've romanticized to a certain extent. We can tell other people, or even ourselves, that we have certain beliefs and convictions, and our intention may genuinely be to uphold that belief. Yet these convictions that you claim to possess exist only in the safety of a pristine emotional vacuum. Honestly, the reality is you don't know, you haven't the foggiest idea. You don't really know what you believe until your beliefs are all you have left. You don't know what your convictions are until they are all you have to hold onto as you've been truly tested.

That's what the Gift of Adversity did for me. Only after going through the fire of Adversity can you even hope to have an inkling of what your convictions are. Only then can you know what you truly believe when nobody's looking. These Priorities are the very foundation upon which everything else in your life worthy of construction will be built.

Adversity = Opportunity

After going through the experience of my injury, it helped me see what a Priority was. Just as importantly, it helped me realize what is not important and why. Things that were of the highest priority one day became merely an afterthought the next. My experience has helped me come to realize the things in my life truly worthy of my focus and energy are the things that mean the world to me. Anything else seems, at best, trivial by comparison.

Determining Priorities

All people have priorities whether they are aware of it or not. Some believe that they must proclaim something a priority as if it must be written down on an "official priority list" in order to be deemed as such. Of course, this is not the case. The things that are a priority to you are the things that you regularly put energy and action towards.

An infant sleeps, eats, and does little else because those are its priorities. A drug addict cares about nothing more but their next fix because that is their priority. A gambler's only priority is the next shot of dopamine they get from winning or almost winning, the next hand or roll of the dice. Though it may go unrecognized, all people have priorities.

When someone isn't clear about what their priorities are this often means the wrong things becomes prioritized. Consequently, things that should be of genuine importance become deprioritized by default. Even when we are clear about our own priorities are, we often become unintentionally sidetracked. The most common way this occurs is because of the priorities of others and the fact that we will put these needs above our own. The priorities of loved ones and/or work jump to the top of this list. The litmus test of what is and is not a priority is simple. To know what someone believes, observe their actions. In order to accomplish the goals you are working towards you must make your priorities the priority. When you can mentally free yourself enough to do this, the thoughts and opinions of others quickly become irrelevant in this endeavor.

I've become much more selective with my time and activities. Throughout my life, I'd always tried to be selfless to avoid being what I perceived to be selfish. I've realized now that it's ok to do things that are more self-centered because if I'm not taking care of myself, it's impossible to help others to the best of my abilities. It's impossible to pour from an empty vessel, and if you don't set boundaries for yourself and continually reinforce them, they are no longer boundaries. They are merely threats and empty ones at that. Self-discipline is nothing more than the ability to follow the carefully crafted plan you have laid out. It's nothing more than being able to follow your own advice— it's holding yourself accountable.

Say No

Through all of this, I've learned to say no, and to say it without guilt or need to justify my answer. If everything is a priority, then nothing is a priority. Start saying no more often. Say no to unnecessary small talk and gossip, but say yes to saying hello and greeting people with sincerity and emotion. Say no to mindlessly scrolling through social media and say yes to reading an article or a book that interests you and adds to your genuine edification. Say no to negative self-talk and say yes to understanding why you deserve to speak respectfully to yourself. Say no to that which you don't truly want and say yes to the things you've always wanted. Say no sooner so that you can say yes, and therefore succeed sooner and more often in the things that are of actual importance.

The things that deserve your greatest effort and focus should only be things that you consider to be truly great. We can do many things over time, but not all at once. Take one thing at a time in order to achieve it exceptionally, and don't expect everything you've ever wanted in life to happen overnight without focused, concentrated work. This allows you more chances to say yes to the things that matter while avoiding endeavors that drain you in the long run. Remember, it's not a priority unless you act like it is.

Returned to Simplicity

We all have clutter in our lives to some extent, from an overflowing email inbox needing attention to drawers full of clothes that you haven't worn in years, there are plenty extraneous things surrounding us every day.

Unfortunately for many of us, we allow this 'acquisition of clutter' mentality to become a habit. This can bleed over into how we deal with other aspects of life. Once the habit is established, the behavior persists and becomes difficult to counter. Then it is no longer an issue of whether or not this clutter is worthy of retention, it is held onto from force of habit. Eventually, these things will swell to become part of a collective chaos. To create order from this chaos will then require time and mental capital that could be better used elsewhere. The reason people have so much clutter in their lives is that they are no longer able to differentiate between what is important from what is not. They have a scarcity mentality, and because of this, they are afraid to let go of anything for the fear that they may realize later that the thing they got rid of was what they needed. By trying to hold on to everything, it makes it impossible to hold onto anything genuinely important. Moreover, they may not even be able to recognize what's of importance in the first place. In turn, this sets them up for failure in the future because they are unable to be selective.

Compelling Goals

"If you are not motivated to act, then your goals simply aren't compelling enough."

-Marcus Aurelius Anderson-

A person is never more productive than when they have purpose. They are never more powerful than when they have a motivation born from something they truly want and desire.

If the goals you are working towards are indeed lofty, then ferocious optimism is what will be needed to achieve them. Without compelling goals, you will lack the drive to engage the work ethic and muster the stamina required to achieve your definition of success. From individual success to ending world hunger, these goals are what will dictate your focus and therefore, attention to that which drives you. Many give up ambition for security and have come to understand that there is no room for security when you are facing the Adversity of achieving your ambitions. I've already died with the regret of not actualizing my goals and priorities twice, I don't intend to do it a third time.

From your list of Priorities, we will reverse engineer and break down the actions required to achieve them. These become your Primary Objectives. Create a short list of your Primary Objectives. Once you start to achieve these objectives one by one, you'll notice something. Once you become focused on achieving the most important things in your life, you'll see that those lesser objectives that you've wanted to work on will, as if by magic, take care of themselves through the power of momentum.

A Gun to Your Head

To make sure the correct things make this Primary Objective list, you must first ask yourself a few questions. Again, brutal honesty is needed here. Ask if the objective you have is something you really want, something you'll truly work hard to achieve. How long are you willing to work for it? Are you willing to sacrifice comfort for it? Would you keep working for it even when you don't seem to be making progress? Will you face Adversity for it? If upon honest closer examination you realize it does not merit being on this list, then scrap it at once. Don't argue. Just chuck it. Yes, get rid of it. Don't even start it, because it will go unfinished, and in the process, you'll have wasted time and intellectual resources on an ultimately fruitless endeavor. It's not worthy of your effort, so stop wasting moments worrying about it and move to the next thing on your list that is worthy of your attention. Every action taken should have a specific purpose. If it does not, it is an action wasted that could've been applied elsewhere.

Think of it this way, if there was a gun to your head and I told you that you had to decide right now this instant if you think that what you're contemplating is or should be a real priority, what would your answer be? I only say this because when it comes to trading your precious time and effort for a goal, it is like a gun to your head. If you are doing something not worthy of your maximum effort, then following it becomes a slow suicide.

When you stop wasting your time doing the garbage you didn't really want to do in the first place, you'll find you're work ethic and effort will increase exponentially. This happens because you're now fully committed to doing the things you genuinely want to accomplish. Having this clear vision is the key to staying focused on the task at hand. Now that we are clear about what your real priorities are, we can begin to strip away the things that are less essential. While this may sound elementary and redundant, hear me out. It is important to identify what is not essential because anything that is a waste of time, mental energy, or peace of mind becomes a distraction and ultimately takes focus from the things that are important in our lives.

Though you now understand what you want to focus on, you may not be aware of the other things that are taking your mental energy from these Priorities. Having this intentional intellectual separation of what you don't need to worry about serves as a queue that keeps your internal dialogue on task without wondering if the option that you currently face is worth worrying about.

Think of it as a focused productivity grocery list. Instead of walking around the grocery store looking at all the stuff that tries to keep you in there longer, and therefore buy more stuff, you can go right to the things you need and get on with your life. If it's not on the list, then you can just move on without another thought. Even if you aren't completely clear on all the things you want in life, you gain a clearer vision by simply getting rid of the junk in your life, that which is unessential.

"It's not the daily increase but daily decrease. Hack away at the unessential."

-Bruce Lee-

There has been so much written about SiJo Lee Jun Fan that I'm almost certain whatever I attempt to add will simply sound like redundant drivel. Nevertheless, I will humbly attempt to add something of substance to the subject of this legendary man.

Lee Jun Fan, better known by his American name Bruce Lee, was the very definition of a Renaissance Man. As an actor he was an absolute cultural icon becoming the prototype of the modern action superstar that is still seen in cinema today. He clearly revolutionized the world of Martial Arts. As an intellectual, he was able to harness the use of mindset and implement it in every area of his life. While there were many who may have thought of combining martial arts, he was one of the few who actually put this philosophy into motion. Perhaps he was emboldened because he was an Asian in the U.S. without fear of recourse from Hong Kong. As a matter of fact, Wing Chun was one of the first recorded mixed martial arts. It is said to be created by a female named Wing Chun. She combined different styles of Gung Fu to create an effective and efficient form of self-defense to teach the monks in the temples who didn't have the luxury of taking a lifetime to learn martial arts. To be able to accomplish what he did in a long lifetime is incredible. When you consider he did all these things in the short 32 years of his life is staggering.

Bruce Lee was what I would call a "Martial Atheist." Though he started his training in Wing Chun Gung Fu initially while in Hong Kong when he came to the United States he began to borrow shamelessly from whatever martial art he researched or encountered. Even if the influence boxing, fencing, or Filipino martial arts wasn't visually apparent to all who observed his fighting application, it was still there as Bruce expressed it in the martial art he created, Jeet Kune Do.

One of the ways Bruce Lee was able to accomplish so much in his life was his ability to find shortcuts or "hack" the subject of Martial Arts, physical development and thinking long before the term was coined in today's culture. One of the overarching concepts that he employed was the idea of decreasing, not increasing. His quote, "I fear not the man who has practiced 10,000 kicks once, but I fear the man who had practiced one kick 10,000 times" exemplifies this attitude beautifully. It is not the number of techniques known that matters, it the quality of how those techniques can be executed that does. This minimalistic ideal is found in other arenas as well.

Pareto Principle

The Pareto Principle, also called the 80/20 ratio, is the observation that 80% of results come from 20% of the effort. Examples of this include:

80% of Pareto's peas in his garden were produced by 20% of his plants.

80% of the work is done by 20% of the employees.

80% of a company's profits come from 20% of their customers.

A great example of this can be found in Boxing. There are plenty of unique punches in Boxing from the shovel and corkscrew hook to switching leads in mid-attack. But of these the most common punches found in boxing gyms are the jab, cross, lead hook, rear hook, lead uppercut, and rear uppercut.

Yet of these six punches, the one that gets the most KO's? The cross.

1 (cross)/6 punches=16.7% which is right line with the 80/20 ratio.

Hick's Law

Hick's Law states that the time it takes to make a decision increases exponentially to the number of choices available. A simple example would be a written test question. The question that has only A and B as answers are easier to answer than a question that has A, B, C and D as answers.

The more answers possible, the longer it takes to find the correct one.

Another real-world example of this can be found in self-defense against a punch. If you learn one effective defense against the right cross, according to Hick's Law you are more likely to be able to execute that single defensive technique than if you know four equally effective counters to the same attack. You would be more likely to successfully perform the one defense you know because you wouldn't have to mentally decide in mid-attack which of the four defenses would be most effective. The amount of time it takes to react knowing four defenses would take four times as long compared to the single defense you have already learned. Having to go through the mental flowchart of which technique to use takes time that you aren't afforded in the heat of battle. Add to that the fear and adrenaline of being attacked and you slow down considerably more.

Another example of simplicity being preferred over complexity is found in Occam's razor. It states that of multiple answers to a question, the simplest answer is generally the correct one. This supposes that the simplest solution generally has the fewest steps, therefore having fewer potentials for error. In a Physics problem, if you can find the desired answer in four steps, according to Occam's razor, this method would be preferred over another method that takes seven steps. The more simply it can be solved, then the lesser the chance for incorrect calculation. All of these examples further illustrate the efficiency of simplicity.

While the minimalistic idea of "less is more" is woven into the fabric of the Asian culture through the philosophies of Taoism, Zen, and Buddhism to name a few, it has only caught on over the last half-century or so in the West.

When encountering a problem, the common response for many is to look for something to add to the situation in the hopes that this will remedy the problem. Generally, this muddies the water making the solution that much harder to ascertain. Many times the solution is to strip away the things unnecessary to the situation instead of overcomplicating it by adding additional variables. Hack away at the unessential. When things don't add up, subtract. Subtract the bullshit. Discard that which is useless. This principle can be employed to strip away everything from unnecessary stress to material items.

Things that were once thought to be a priority that is now known to be superfluous should be eliminated.

Am I saying that you can't have a big beautiful house, a luxurious car or expensive clothing? Absolutely not. You can have all those things and more if you so desire. What I am asking is this: when do you have enough?

My point is that if you don't have a vision or idea of what is enough, if you don't know what you are after, then the default answer is always going to be to have more. If you constantly want more, you will gradually come to understand that anything in excess eventually becomes their opposite. How?

I'll give you an excellent example of a social custom found throughout the world. It's called dating.

Say you meet person A at a coffee shop. You hit it off and end up exchanging numbers. Later that same evening at the gym person B, who you've always found attractive, asks to get a bite to eat after your workout. The dinner goes well, and you agree to meet up again next week. On your way to work the next day, person C comes up and asks you for directions. You have a great conversation, and they text you shortly after to thank you again. Meanwhile at work the following day, you meet the new co-worker who smiles openly at you, though the company handbook states in detail that there is to be no fraternization with person D.

Because you now have three other people texting and calling you, it takes more of your mental focus. And of course, now they want even more of your free time socially. The new co-worker, who you're not to fraternize with, asks you to go fraternize after work on Friday. Of the four people, they all have components that you enjoy immensely. You connect on many levels with each of them and some more than others.

Person A is just an enjoyable person to be around. Person B you have a more physical attraction to than the others. Person C is very genuine and who doesn't like that? And your co-worker, person D, is possibly just the forbidden fruit that attracts you because they are off limits.

Eventually, the entire dance becomes rather laborious. Person A is becoming a bit too desperate. Person B has become incredibly high maintenance. Person C is slightly passive aggressive; and between all of them, your phone is always lit up. This amount of incoming texts doesn't go unseen by the co-worker you've been spending ever more time with, and they confront you about it at work no less. When pressed about it you tell them that you aren't exclusive, though they inform you that they thought you were. They are not pleased, to say the least.

It becomes even more uncomfortable when Person A see's you out with Person B when you told them earlier that you were going to stay in for the night. Just then person C texts to tell you they have a death in the family, and you feel obligated to be there for them, though the timing couldn't be worse. The next day your co-worker's cold shoulder is apparent as are the daggers darting from their eyes. You also have a visit from your boss who needs to see you-something about a complaint about harassment of a co-worker.

As you can see, anything in excess eventually becomes their opposite. While the initial hope was to find a person to date, when too many are put into the mix, the end result is often disastrous. I also understand that there are many ways to use communication to remedy this particular example, but the idea of excess becoming the opposite of the original intent is the point I'm illustrating. The same goes for information.

Unknowns

Life is full of unknowns. Honestly, there is very little that we really know or understand about our world completely. Most of us know a small amount about a number of things that we interact with from day to day.

Now I ask you this: how much do we really want to know? In the grand scheme of things, must we know every little thing about everything we interact with? Must I know every individual mechanism of my cell phone to be able to use it?

Sometimes minimalism is all that's requisite. For example, let's say my car breaks down and I'm miles from the nearest town. Even if I understand the mechanical problem with my vehicle, unless I have the parts, tools, and time required to fix it, it does little to help my vehicle run again at the moment. The point being, I for one don't need or even want to know the mechanism of every single thing I interact with. There is too much information, and all that static would take up way too much of my time, effort, and memory in the long run. I would rather reserve that potential mental capacity to do other things. The lesson being we shouldn't clog up our mind with useless facts and tidbits that, in the long run, are virtually worthless. The reality is we have precious little time and a finite amount of mental energy to do the things that are worthy of our attention, so we must be very selective and choose wisely. The modern information age with constant push notifications, messages, and updates has created a type of built-up anxiety of attrition that is becoming rampant. There is a genuine sensory overload phenomenon that is occurring in modern society. Sensory overload has the following symptomology:

Inability to focus on a single task

Difficulty concentrating

Sleepiness/Fatigue

Irritability

Exhibits difficulty in social interactions

Sound familiar? Do you recognize this behavior in anyone you know? Perhaps even in yourself?

This self-inflicted form of sensory overload is now omnipresent in today's culture. When overwhelmed with information, the mind seeks a break from this overload as a sort of defense mechanism. This is another reason why distractions are so sought out in society today. There is a multi-billion-dollar economy based solely on distractions that keep people willfully artificially pacified.

In today's social media fed, internet-driven mentality and lifestyle, people are losing the ability for linear thinking. Many in this generation will not read an entire paragraph but simply scan it looking for pertinent data that jumps out at them. While this is good if you're just looking for a few keywords, in the long run, it takes more time. Finding a keyword does little to define its context. Therefore you have to go back to hunt and seek to understand the information that you need, taking even more time the second time to read and process the information. The effect from this 'scanning for information' instead of reading can be seen which results in shorter abilities to concentrate.

These changes in attention span are now being reflected in advertisements. Many commercials will rest on an image or a scene for little more than a second or two before switching images. Advertisers are also smart in understanding their audience when creating a commercial. If it's for a younger demographic, they will use the previously mentioned 'strobe light' marketing technique to keep up with the dwindling attention of that generation. Conversely, when they are looking for the more mature (older, grew up without a cell phone and internet) demographic they will often have one or perhaps two wide shots and have the commercial unfold within those confines.

This reduction of linear thinking affects people's ability express themselves verbally as well as the written word. This means that many people aren't having necessarily deep intellectual conversations but are instead simply regurgitating information that they have just heard or seen most recently.

While this allows them the ability to parrot others quotes and ideology, it does little in allowing them the opportunity to contemplate the meaning of said philosophy. It also gives them less of an independent mindset, discouraging their natural curiosity to question everything. While being able to quote certain people readily and having neatly trimmed soundbites at your disposal may sound momentarily impressive, it does little to allow you to contemplate and find deeper meaning within yourself. This thin minded mentality and thought process does little for any forward progress in the individual. As Einstein said, "imagination is more important than knowledge," and though we have much more of the latter, it is causing the slow elimination the former.

"I cultivate empty space as a way of life for the creative process."

-Josh Waitzkin-

Stripping

The concept of saying no and stripping away the unessential go hand in hand. Understand that the stripping away of inessentials is a way of lightening your load that you are burdened with, every small thing that you don't need doesn't seem like it weighs much, but when it's all added together, it can weigh a ton. Big things are made up of a bunch of small things all put together. Learn to let go of the thoughts that don't serve you, let go of the ones that are a burden. If they don't help you, then rid yourself of their cognitive and emotional dead weight. We never know which small straw will break the metaphorical camel's back. We can start by going through the clothing in your closet. If it has been an entire season or an entire year and you haven't worn that article of clothing or haven't had a need to wear it, do you really need it?

Use this mentality when it comes to meetings, phone calls, emails and text messages. If you're in the middle of doing something and in the flow of productivity, turn your phone off and block out all distractions until you get what you want to get it done. Think of these example as a way to keep you selfish and stingy with your time and focus; there are so many things in life that try to steal it from you, don't fall victim to these thieves of focus.

Take this stripping away from the inessential's concept and apply to other things in your life such as relationships and social interactions. Ask yourself if the conversation you're about to engage in is necessary? There's no reason to be outright rude, however, make choices to decide who you want to engage with and what is more of a distraction than an improvement to what it is you're trying to accomplish.

Do the same thing with your thoughts. Stop tolerating your own internal dialogue that allows you to think unnecessary and negative things. Strip away the inessential thoughts that do not make you stronger and happier. Allow the thoughts that do not bring you peace to fall away from your mentality and mindset. This is the entire concept of meditation, to let thoughts come and go without expectation or attachment.

Letting go of anger and having forgiveness is another form of hacking away at inessential. The word 'forgive' when broken down = for + give. It means you're giving emotion for something. In this case, the emotion you're giving is the feeling of anger or hate. You are giving the feeling away, simply letting it go. In exchange FOR the negativity, you are GIVING yourself peace and closure. While this is easy to say, many don't know how to break this cognitive cycle. The way to do this to have goals and ideas that lead you and to make a conscientious decision to stay mentally engaged on these things only. Use the knowledge that multitasking is a waste of time. Therefore, we should have a sole focus on our goals daily.

Chapter VI

Know Thyself

"War's not as bad as you think, it's worse than you can ever imagine."

-SSG Basil Reid-

What Gets Men Killed

Staff Sergeant Basil Reid is a warrior in every sense of the word, and I'd never use such a term lightly. After six deployments between the Marines and the Army, SSG Reid has been deployed for a longer amount of time than most combat veteran's total time of service in the military. I consider myself very lucky to have had a man of his caliber as my squad leader while I was stationed at 10th Mountain.

While training room clearing (entering a room by force and engaging enemy combatants) he gave me some incredibly valuable advice that I keep in mind to this day. Between iterations, the squad dashes to our rally point in the wood line about 15 meters from the shoot houses. SSG Reid lights a cigarette with his battle-worn Zippo as our squad sits down under the midnight Upstate New York summer sky. After taking a long drag off his cigarette he asks me, "A.J.

do you know what gets more men killed in battle than bullets, grenades, and IED's?" He gave me a moment to contemplate this as the cigarette smoke slowly escaped his exhalation. I took a drink of water out of my Camel Back and wiped the sweat from my brow as I pondered his question. After training with this man for some time, I'd learned quickly that I knew very little when it came to military combat. SSG Reid had led our squad through the intricacies and necessity of trench warfare. He showed the importance of squad movements, having us do these at night, even while the rest of the platoon slept. He taught me the most effective fieldcraft for long-distance marksmanship, ambushing, tracking, demolition, and reconnaissance. Even with my extensive martial arts background, he showed me incredibly efficient techniques using a knife as well as hand to hand combat. What I was currently learning from him regarding room clearing was gold. Combat theory is important to understand, but this man has the experience to back it up. While some leaders will hide behind theories found in a book, he had the combat wisdom to throw theory out the window when it made no sense and became cumbersome. SSG Reid taught us time and again how violence of action, mental toughness, and the sheer will to survive may be the only things that get you and your squad back alive more than theory ever could. SSG Reid had enough firsthand knowledge in multiple forms of combat to fill volumes, and I soaked up as much of it as possible. As he finished his cigarette, recognizing that I had no good answer, he continued: *"The thing that gets more men killed in battle than anything else? Indecision."*

His answer instantly made sense to me. He smirked as he saw the recognition of the lesson on my face. He expounded on his point, "If you are leading men, it's better to make the wrong decision than to be undecided because when you are undecided, you are standing still. When you are standing still, you're an easy target and as good as dead, but if you make a decision, even the wrong one, you still have a chance to correct it as you go. You can make a choice decisively, realize that you're wrong while on the move and course correct on the fly. Doing this gives you a much better chance not only of survival but of accomplishing the objective in front of you that if you stand still, too unsure to act." He added: "Remember that the battle is always changing, it's never static. Intel can be and often is wrong. Strategies will change based on the actions of the enemy while targets of opportunity may also present themselves. You must be able to adapt to this in a heartbeat. Even the best plan falls apart quickly under pressure. Everyone has a plan until they make contact. As soon as the first shot is fired, everything can go to hell in a hurry. So, you might as well get used to learning to adapt to being wrong now instead of in the chaos of the fight, because in combat, sooner or later, the chaos will find you." The resonance of truth in this lesson echoes in many areas of life. When you're in combat, there is always going to be risk and danger present, but as SSG Reid points out so well, the greatest risk lies in trying to avoid the Adversity. This leads to the hesitation that creates indecision, and ultimately death for the soldier. It's no coincidence that books like "The Art of War," "The Book of Five Rings," and other classic works based on the tactics of war are found so often on the bookshelves of countless CEO's and successful entrepreneurs.

There are many parallels and similarities between warfare and modern business, and reading these texts give tremendous insight. One of the most successful entrepreneurs to echo SSG Reid's sentiment in the world of business is none other than Facebook creator Mark Zuckerberg: "The biggest risk is not taking any risk. In a world that's changing really quickly, the only strategy that is guaranteed to fail is not taking risks."

Learn to dance with the fear and the risk; because if what you want is worth having, then the fear never goes away entirely.

Purpose

There's a reason soldiers have been able to endure risks and overcome insurmountable odds to achieve victory for centuries. It comes down to one thing: Purpose.

This Purpose is born from the soldier's Priorities. These are the things he loves and holds dear: The idea of defending his family and country, his sense of duty and honor. Fighting for these priorities and for those who fight by his side are the things that keep the soldier's efforts concentrated. The knowledge that this single-minded focus gives him is what makes him fight on against all the odds. While in battle, he can strip away all distractions in order to face his foe with all of his capacities and intent. The ability to fight without the inhibition of indecision gives the soldier the greatest chance of victory over Adversity. This is why it is imperative to take the time to decide what your Priorities really are. By knowing what a Priority is, we can begin breaking it down into actionable steps that lead to Purpose.

Your PURPOSE is your mission.

The VISION is the game plan that is created based on this Purpose.

The PRIMARY OBJECTIVES are the goals that come from reverse engineering your Vision.

Once your Primary Objectives are established, all that is left to do is apply every ounce your focus and energy towards making these goals into reality no matter what.

Even when the situation changes for a soldier, the Priorities stay the same. The plans may change, but the mission is resolute. There is no fatigue, weather conditions, lack of food and water, or fear that is going to impede him from fighting with everything that he has to overcome that which lies before him.

By having this purpose already preconceived and decided, there is never a question of what should be accomplished from moment to moment. This singular purpose is the internal mantra that is subconsciously repeated throughout the mission keeping him focused and on task. The thing that drives us forward is purpose. Without purpose, we become the victim of hesitation. And like those who hesitate in combat, it usually worsens our situation. The plan may change, but the Priority and Purpose are constant and unwavering.

Priorities – Distractions/Inessential = Purpose

What is My True Purpose?

Everyone has asked this question at some point in their lives. Many have asked this question multiple times as their lives change and evolve. Some may even ask it from day to day. This is obviously a huge question to ask, let alone answer. It can be even more overwhelming when you take into consideration that everything else you do in your life is based on this one question. This is the very reason most will avoid giving the question any serious consideration, because it's intimidating to admit to yourself, "I don't know."

Understand that there are millions of others, including myself, who have set forward on a well thought out and definitive path only to find out that they would have to radically change their route. This detour is often in the complete opposite direction from where they initially ventured, due to things outside of their control. There are 50-year-olds who still don't know what they want to be when they "grow up." That's why it will come as a relief when you realize that every successful person, be it an athlete, actor, musical artist or entrepreneur, was at one time unsure of what their future held as well. It's okay not to know. In fact, it's the norm, and it's all part of the process.

"You must understand that there is more than one path to the top of the mountain."

-Miyamoto Musashi-

When deciding your destination, it needs to be done from a place of honesty and not out of a place of fear. Making a decision based on fear does nothing but lead to more negativity in the future. This creates a cycle of fear, anxiety and inevitably more bad decisions. Step back for a moment and take a deep breath. Realize that there is not one singular profession or pursuit you must do to be completely fulfilled. It's not as if there is only one specific route that must be taken to find happiness, success, and satisfaction.

If we decide to follow a path that eventually dead ends, so be it. It's not as if it's "right" or "wrong," it's an experience that gives us information. Think of it as a way of collecting data that can later be analyzed and applied to future endeavors, this time with more experience.

Even if you feel stuck in your current employment or career, know that you still have options and alternatives. Many things work, so work many things. There are thousands of ways to success; you just have to find the way that works best for you.

There are many paths to the top of the mountain. It matters not which one we take, what matters is that we are pressing ever towards the summit. What matters is that we commit to a decision, the rest will follow from this. Remember the words of SSG Reid and a deeper lesson that they hold: In this life, hesitation doesn't just kill men, it kills dreams and ambitions as well. Take your time to make an honest, informed decision, but decide. Commit fully to that the path; then you can reevaluate as necessary.

"You can fail at what you don't want, so you might as well take a chance on doing what you love."

-Jim Carrey-

Ikigai

Because this is a very complicated and multifaceted question, it's important to break it down into smaller pieces to make it easier to digest.

The word ikigai (pronounced E-Key-Guy) comes from two words. Iki which means 'life, alive' and kai (voiced as gai) meaning 'result, worth, benefit.' Ikigai roughly translates to "reason for being" in Japanese. For many of us, this is how we define Purpose. From the graphic, you can see the four sphere's that shape each person's ikigai. The top sphere consists of the things you love to do. Moving clockwise the next sphere is made up of what the world needs. The bottom sphere is comprised of the things you can be paid to do. The final sphere is composed of the things you do well. Take a moment to reflect and write in the 3-5 things that fit into each of the 4 spheres in your personal ikigai. As you notice the areas that the spheres overlap are also significant. These areas of overlap give you an indication of Mission, Vocation, Profession, and Passion. Much like these overlapping ideas, you'll see how the 3-5 things that you wrote into each sphere will have areas of overlap or potentials of overlap. The center where these spheres overlap is considered your personal ikigai or "reason for being."

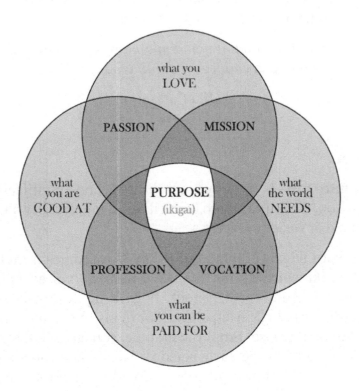

Temet Nosce

Doing this exercise is important because it helps you see written in black and white what your strengths are and potentials for where those strengths lie. It gives you an overhead view that allows not only perspective but candor as well. There may be things that you know you are good at, and there may also be things that you aren't aware of that you are good at that you may take for granted. Honestly, there may be things that you think you're good out, but in reality, you are not. There is a phenomenon known as Rothbard's Law.

The economist Murray Rothbard stated: "People tend to specialize in what they're worst at." While the statement was made somewhat sardonically, it still has a tremendous amount of observational truth to it.

The issue it exposes is this: we seem to take the things we do well for granted. Take a person who is naturally gifted at the complex mathematics of Calculus. Because this subject comes easily to them, the fact that there are many who may find the subject difficult and challenging will seem confusing to them. From their viewpoint, they can't understand why anyone would have trouble with something as simple as Calculus. Much like an actor who wants to be taken seriously for their political opinions, they are essentially expounding on a subject in which they have little expertise.

Everyone understands the need to improve in the areas we are lacking, but the notion of constantly improving our weaknesses coupled with Rothbard's Law often distracts us from embracing the things we are good at doing.

Serial entrepreneur Gary Vaynerchuk mentions the necessity for "self-awareness" as a cornerstone of success in both business and life. He states that the key to finding the job you love is to hone in on your biggest strengths and skillsets. He suggests that you ask people who know you well to give you an honest opinion of both your strengths and weaknesses.

In an earlier chapter, I spoke of the need to be brutally honest with yourself when finding your true priorities. This brutal honesty is what allows ferocious optimism for your future.

The phrase "gnothi seauton" in Greek and the more familiar Latin version "temet nosce" both roughly translate in English to mean the same thing: Know Thyself. Socrates' famous proclamation that "people make themselves appear ridiculous when they are trying to know obscure things before they know themselves" is a great lesson in the necessity of brutal honesty when evaluating ourselves. Whether you call it self-awareness, brutal honesty or to know thyself, the important thing to realize is that this truth has been studied and discussed for centuries for a good reason. It is this self-knowledge that helps us make the best decisions possible regarding the future.

You will find there are things in life that you are good at and enjoy. These are the things that you will naturally gravitate towards. Many times, it is a combination of all these experiences coupled with your natural gifts and attributes that will form your best choices in life.

Even if you don't come to know your exact purpose at this very moment, the simple act of asking these questions and filling out your ikigai is enough to set you well on your way to doing so. You will also find that your purpose will change with time.

Perhaps your initial goal is to have a successful business, but once you've achieved that, what next? After you've bought all the material things you've always wanted and been to all the cool, exotic vacation spots, then what? This is a perfect example of what happens when a person has no vision. Like before, if you have no vision, then the answer is always going to be to chase after "more." This shows how important it is to have vision built into your purpose.

"One day you will wake up, and there won't be any more time to do the things you've always wanted. Do it now."

-Paulo Coelho-

You may live to be 100 years old, or you may die as you're reading this. The point is you don't know, and that is both the beauty and tragedy of this thing called life. I always thought I'd have time because up to the point of my injury, I did. Don't squander the time you've been given because there are no guarantees in this life.

Parkinson's Law

Parkinson's Law is the adage that states: "Work expands to fill the time available for its completion."

If you are given a deadline of two days to get something done, guess how long it will take? Usually two days. But what if it's a task that only takes about six hours of work, how long will it take you to get it done if you have a two-day deadline? Usually two days.

Now take the same task that you can get done comfortably in six hours, but now you must finish it in five hours. If you take the deadline seriously, even if you have to work harder to achieve it, magically it is finished in the allotted time. Amazing.

A similar situation presented itself as I write this book. Deadlines have been moved up time and again, and yet you are reading it now. This is another great example of Parkinson's Law. If you don't allow room for the task to expand and you must compress the work to fit into the timeframe given, you'll be amazed at what can be achieved.

I'm sure everyone has experienced this phenomenon at some point. This is the very reason written assignments have a hard deadline. That's also why there are so many who finish their paper in at the 11th hour of the deadline given. Use Parkinson's Law as a way to create your best work in regard to your Purpose and Primary Objectives. It will force you to focus and compress your efforts, saving you time and mental energy in the long run.

Nothing gives you a greater sense of urgency than knowing two things:

1. *Your purpose*

2. *That you have an unknown but limited amount of time to accomplish your purpose.*

Knowing that your life has an expiration date and that you now know the things you want to accomplish within that timeframe should give you laser-like focus. This is the very definition of a deadline, the deadline of your life. This deadline is approaching whether you accomplish your goals or not, so you need to do everything in your power to accomplish as much as you possibly can in the time you have left. Without a deadline, time means nothing.

Think about the stories of people who are diagnosed with a terminal illness and only given a year to live. Notice how that creates a sense of urgency in them knowing that their life is short? That's why they spend the next six months or a year trying to pack in everything they ever wanted to do into what's left of their lifetime. Wouldn't you live your life differently if you knew you were dying? Well, you are. We all are, actually. To live as if you are dying creates a life worth living, regardless of how much time you may have left.

Your future beckons. Embrace it with all your might and fight for that which you want for as long as there is a breath of life within you. Then when you're on your deathbed, you will lie there with no regrets, no fears only found reflections of satisfaction. And in this life, that's all we could ever ask for.

Marathon of Purpose

Think of the legendary runner at the Battle of Marathon. What made that messenger run with such speed? Purpose. Strong, definitive, single-minded purpose.

As the massive Persian army was landing their ships outside the city of Marathon, the Greeks knew they would need help if they had any hope of defending their city. Being heavily outnumbered and underequipped, they assigned a messenger with an incredible responsibility: to run as fast as his legs could carry him the 26.2 miles from Marathon to Athens to get reinforcements. To get this message delivered as quickly as possible was a matter of life and death. It was for the runner as well, because according to legend, he died soon after delivering that message.

When you find your purpose, you will have a burning desire much as this runner did. A message that you are willing to put your life on the line for. A message you are willing to die trying to deliver. Find your purpose. Find your message. Find your Marathon, then run like hell.

My Purpose to Walk Again

"A man can only be beaten in two ways. If he gives up, or if he dies."

-Richard Machowicz-

After now viewing my Adversity as a gift, I accepted the fact that I was going to have to work harder than I had ever before to even have a chance of regaining my ability to walk. I had pushed my body to the limit and beyond time and again previously, but this was uncharted territory. I had to make peace with the notion that even after I had given everything I could possibly give, there was still no guarantee that I'd be able to walk or use my hands again. Be that as it may, I committed wholeheartedly to the process. I was an empty vessel ready to be filled with potential. Days went by and nothing happened. Days turned into weeks with no change. After a month of trying, I was still exactly the same. Even so, I remained focused and undaunted.

When you are in a bed unable to move, for better or worse, you watch a lot of Netflix. I would have someone start up from where I'd last left off in the TV series and I'd be good for a few hours at least. The remote was placed next to my bed on a table.

As I'm watching the end credits of the episode start to roll, I really didn't feel like watching the next episode. As I thought this, subconsciously I must have tried to pick up the remote. My left hand tingled and I could see my fingers move ever so slightly. It wasn't a much movement mind you, but it was definitive. I tried again and could reproduce the action. I continued this five more times until I wasn't able to again.

I was in shock, in the best possible way. I tried to move the rest of my body to no avail, but I was still overjoyed with this simple finger flexion and extension, no matter how minute it may have been. I tried to suppress my excitement in fear that I may set myself up for a greater emotional fall in the future like before. No matter. Such a small gesture gave me more happiness than I'd experienced in 6 months! For this brief moment in time, I was allowing myself this small potential victory. And yes, I had that stupid grin on my face the rest of the evening.

The next morning at my PT appointment, I told my therapist about what had happened, and she was still very cautious about her optimism. We had both been down this road before, and she knew the devastating effect it had on me previously. I tried to move my fingers again to show her, but as before, I was unable to cause any movement. She told me to be patient and stay the course. And so I did for the next four months.

Slowly, both hands began to regain movement. Then some arm movement here and there. It was slow, but it was happening. The toes and feet began to move eventually as well. I didn't push it; I exercised aggressive patience to keep from losing any of the new ground I was regaining. It was still going to be a long road. There were days where I seemed to improve, others where I didn't seem to progress at all. The worst days were the ones where I lost ground, but nevertheless, I kept pushing with all I had, because at the moment, this fight was all I had.

Even when my entire body was able to move somewhat, I was still a long way from being able to hold a glass of water, eat with a fork, or walk. Having grotesque body motion was one thing, and while it was better than what I was before, regaining fine motor skills was even more challenging. It was also impossible to know to what degree I'd be able to regain my motor skills. Each day I told myself: "If this is as much movement as I have for the rest of my life, at least I'm better off than I was a few months ago." I'd be lying to you if I told you I wasn't hoping like mad that I'd come back good as new.

The human spinal cord is very fragile and delicate. It is comprised of a large bundle of nerves from ½ to ¼ inch in diameter depending on what region of the spine you are in.

When seeing a cross-section of the spinal cord with the naked eye, it looks like a bundle of small rubber bands all bunched together running horizontally around 17-18 inches in length. Every nerve in your body from the tips of your fingers and toes to your heart, lungs and every other organ in your body originates from here. The spinal cord with the brain creates the central nervous system, the master system that controls everything from your immune system to your ability to smell fresh honeysuckle in the summer.

This delicate structure is protected by the bony armor surrounding it, the spine. The spine is made up of vertebra that are stacked on top of each other like building blocks contouring to the spinal cord in size and creating curves to allow better shock absorption. The discs between the vertebras are like large jelly donuts, hard on the outside and filled with a thick gel on the inside. These structures serve as shock absorbers as well and have the density of a hockey puck.

I say all this to paint a vivid picture. Some people may have a bulging disc in their spine, but there are varying degrees of this. When a disc bulges it can create pressure on the spinal cord. It only takes 10 millimeters of mercury pressure (mmHg) to compromise a nerve, especially the big bundle of nerves in the spine. To give you an idea of how much 10 mmHg weighs, it's the approximate weight of a dime. The disc bulge can worsen and potentially herniate. Disc herniation, like disc bulges, vary by degrees as well. When the disc in my neck herniated, it was a complete rupture. The disc exploded. This meant that the pressure of that thick, dense intervertebral disc pressed back onto my spinal cord. It created a tremendous amount of pressure, like a hockey puck pressing down and choking the life out of me. Far greater than the weight of a dime to say the least.

The pressure was so great that you could see on my MRI that there was zero cerebral spinal fluid moving below the level of injury. Like a garden hose that was stepped on, without this fluid, the spinal cord couldn't function. There are limitations of matter. The body can heal itself to an extent, but it must have something to work with. For example, with time the body can heal a broken finger. However, if that finger is cut off, the body is unable to regrow a new finger due to limitations of matter.

Similarly, a diabetic may have a pancreas, but due to limitations of matter, the pancreas cannot produce enough insulin consistently and repeatedly to stabilize the person's blood sugar levels. Thus, the need for the diabetic to take insulin.

Live to Tell

All the tests performed showed that I had a tremendous amount of neurological damage. So much so that I shouldn't even be able to do the things that I was already doing.

The thing about dying and living to tell the tale is that you learn quickly what is truly important to you. One of the most important things I learned from my injury is that you have no time to waste and you have absolutely nothing to lose. I was told I'd never walk again, let alone be able to feed myself, type on a computer, or text on a cell phone. While I still was far from being able to do these things, I maintained the cautious optimism that had already gotten me farther than the doctors ever thought I'd reach. My thoughts were that if I can do these things that they said I'd never be able to do already, then what's to stop me from proving them all wrong by doing everything else and more? Now revitalized, I was going to push to the limitations of matter and beyond as much a humanly possible. I had found my Marathon.

People say that life is a Marathon and not a sprint. In reality, life is a collection of both paces, often changing from one pace to the other in an instant. This is how my recovery was. It was a Marathon, a Marathon of sprints.

Distracted Much?

"Most people want a distraction from their lives. As for me, I've created a life that doesn't make me seek distraction."

-Marcus Aurelius Anderson-

There are countless distractions around us all the time. When a person becomes distracted, many times, they aren't even aware of it. Why? Because they're distracted! Most are never more in search of a distraction than when they are working an hourly job. People check out social media while at work for fifteen minutes which turns into half an hour. Let's say they do this twice a day equaling 1-hour a day. If they do this five days a week, that equals 20 hours in a month totaling 240 hours a year! If that same person works a 40-hour week, that means they've wasted the equivalent of 6 WEEKS OF BEING UNPRODUCTIVE at work because of this small' DISTRACTION'!

If you are an entrepreneur, then the price is even higher because your time is much more valuable than just the hourly wage of a person who works 9 to 5. A person checks social media for 'just a second'. Then they see a post or story that grabs their attention, and they become completely enthralled. They get lost in it, and before they realize, they've wasted a ton of time, and they've lost more than just that one hour of productively in that work day. How? They lose more time because they've lost the momentum and focus they had previously, and because they became distracted, they've shifted their mindset and thinking entirely. Now, it could take another five or ten minutes just to get back into the same sort of focus and single-minded thought patterns requisite to create their best productivity. Take into consideration the way you FEEL after reading an aggravating story or post. You FEEL angry, sad, and disappointed but more than anything, you STILL FEEL distracted because you are unfocused on the task at hand. This mental aggravation can sabotage your ability to refocus on the previous task and bother you possibly for the rest of the day.

So that '15 minutes' wasted on social media (which is 30 minutes) done twice a day has doubled meaning you've lost at least two hours of productivity. Adjusting the numbers for the two hours of lost productivity creates 12 WEEKS OF lost productivity!!

Listen, the mindset of a person who just works an hourly 9-to-5 job is different than a person who is their own boss, business owner, or entrepreneur. Many hourly employees are watching the clock and often trying to just pass the time. This potential three months of "paid vacation while on the job" is not a big deal to them because they're still getting paid for it!

But, if you own the business and allow yourself this small social media distraction, this means you have 12 weeks where you were not being productive and essentially, NOT GETTING PAID!! You won't be in business long if you keep doing that.

Always remember: Time is finite; distraction is infinite. Since time is finite, we must make the most of our productivity in all areas. Discipline yourself to stay within that mental zone, to focus just a little bit longer on the task while you were still warmed up and in that headspace. You'll come to realize you can get more done in 15 minutes of concentrated and focused productivity than in an hour of distracted multitasking busywork that is fruitless in the end. Time is a luxury that we cannot produce.

There is no greater motivation than realizing you have been given a second chance. After reading this and committing to act, everything you do from this moment forward is a second chance for you as well. Do not squander it.

Are You Normal?

Acting like a "normal person" with a "normal work ethic" "normal motivation" and "normal attention span" will get you "normal" results. Normal is unoriginal, often subpar, and flat out boring. I'd wager that your biggest dreams and desires don't involve things that are "normal," subpar, or boring. So how in the hell can a "normal" mentality create the things that you've always wanted in your life? It can't, and to think any differently is the very definition of insanity. Don't be "normal." Choose to be abnormal. Have abnormal expectations of yourself. Have an abnormal work ethic and focus if you want to achieve things that are above and beyond what is the norm.

Listen, whatever you've been doing up to this point in your life if you're honest with yourself, you know you can give more. You know you can try harder and ask more of yourself than what you're currently doing. We both know it. The reason you aren't shifting to those higher gears that are still inside you is that you haven't had a reason to engage that next level. You have become comfortable, and comfort is the enemy of ambition.

Willfully seek out the thing that we all know makes you work harder, push further, and demand more from yourself. Set a deadline. Create a Primary Objective. Make a commitment.

You know the thing I'm talking about, don't act like you don't. You know it by name: Adversity.

Focus

In our day to day lives, it is hard to escape interruptions and vicarious distractions. Sometimes they are unavoidable.

When you find yourself caught up in distraction, stop and acknowledge it. Don't judge or scold yourself for it, simply go back to your focused work. If you mentally beat yourself up about it, it will cause more internal aggravation creating a negative emotional loop that you will now need to overcome. This will take more time and effort in the long run and is another example of how stripping away is the better solution than becoming upset at yourself for being a distraction.

Here are two different scenarios regarding acknowledging and dealing with mental distraction:

Situation #1: You become distracted. You become mentally aware that you are distracted. This angers you because you now feel that you lack discipline. This recognition creates more internal turmoil because this seems to be a pattern you've seen in other things as well. It's as if you have a hard time concentrating on many things, which makes you think of a conversation you had earlier with your significant other who said that weren't focused enough. You now become even more aggravated. Well, who are they to say that? It's not as if they are perfect! They don't know all the pressure and stress you are under every day! They don't know how sleep deprived you are!

Well, that escalated quickly.

Situation #2: You become distracted. You become mentally aware that you are distracted. You acknowledge it. You don't dwell on it. You get back in the groove.

This focus is much like meditation. When beginning meditation, you learn that it can be hard to stay focused, especially when you start out. As you gain more experience with it, this lessons to a degree, but it will be more of a challenge on some days more than others. If you can stay focused for 15 minutes to empty your mind or focus on a singular thought while remaining in a calm seated position, it will make your concentration in any other area of your daily life that much more focused. This is the very reason why people meditate because it helps them learn to stay focused on what they are trying to accomplish in that moment.

Everyone has times when they fall off and lose focus, but to make progress, you must allow yourself these shortfalls from time to time. Becoming distracted and deciding to just give up on being productive for the rest of the afternoon can be tempting. This would be similar to getting a flat tire, then getting out of the car and slashing another tire; because why not, you've already got a flat anyway, right?

By having your Primary Objectives always in mind, it helps you stay focused on the task at hand. This keeps you from becoming distracted and also helps you refocus when you do indeed become distracted. The question you should ask yourself is this: Are you going to let this distraction keep you from accomplishing your goal? Yeah, I didn't think so either.

The Layover Concept

I learned a great lesson while on a layover at the Logan International Airport in Boston waiting for a connecting flight to New York City. It was late January in Boston, and the frigid Northeastern winter was wreaking havoc on all transportation in the city, especially aircrafts.

A woman's voice came on over the speaker in the standing room only waiting area, "Our connecting flight to New York City has been canceled due to adverse weather conditions. We apologize for the inconvenience."

A collective groan emerged from the crowd. That was the third time we'd heard a similar announcement over the last seven hours of watching and waiting. The flight had been delayed multiple times, but unfortunately, this was the final connecting flight out to New York City that evening. All the local hotels I'd tried to email or call earlier were already booked, and even if I could get a room, finding ground transportation at 11:21 PM to get there would be a nightmare in this weather. This meant that I would get to spend the night on a cold, uncomfortable sofa in the airport and hope that the flight in the early morning wasn't delayed as well.

I was aggravated, but not necessarily because of the weather. The weather is something that can't be helped. I was aggravated at myself for not anticipating the issues with the weather. I was more aggravated because originally I had anticipated the possibility of bad weather, but I'd gone against my gut instinct. When I was looking for flights months before, I saw a direct flight that I was going to book. Then I saw a flight with one layover that saved me almost $250 in the same timeframe I'd selected. By booking this flight with only one connecting flight, I'd save myself enough money to pay for my hotel in NYC, seemed like a win, win. You can imagine my surprise.

As I tried to settle in and get "comfy" on the sofa I'd been able to secure, a thought kept running through my mind:

"Damn, I'd gladly pay the extra $250 I saved to be in a warm hotel bed at my destination right about now."

This is the Layover Concept, and it is a great lesson about value, specifically the value of time compared to money. Still unable to get warm or comfortable on the sofa, the value of time vs. money became painfully obvious to me: Money is worthless compared to time. It seems everyone wants to have money, but few want to work hard or endure for any appreciable length of time to gain it.

When we are young, the desire to earn money is a big motivator. You feel you have a large commodity of this resource called time; it isn't as precious to you as the thing that you don't have as much of and desire, money. As you get a bit older, you realize that money is important, but so is time. They have equal weight in deciding what you will commit to, so paying money and applying your time are the both seem to have value.

As you grow even wiser, you realize that time is your greatest asset and commodity. The law of supply and demand aligns well with this example. At this level of thinking, you understand that time is always finite and therefore in short supply because it cannot be created. Much like buying land, the supply is limited, but the demand is ever expanding.

Our time is limited, but our capacity to make money will always be there, in one way or another. Money can be made, time cannot. Even a young person knows that time is more precious than money.

Here's an example:

If you ask a new college graduate what they would rather have, their current age and college debt or to be a multimillionaire but 75 years old, they will choose their youth every single time.

This illustrates my point splendidly: If you are not willing to give up the next 40-50 years of your life for millions of dollars, then what does that tell you about the importance of time? Furthermore, how valuable does that make this moment?

"Trying to be happy by accumulating possessions is like trying to satisfy hunger by taping sandwiches all over your body."

-George Carlin-

The Hedonic Treadmill Theory states that a person stays at a relatively consistent and stable level of happiness regardless of goals achieved, an increase of salary, and acquisition of material riches. Think about your ultimate dream vehicle, the one that to you is the epitome of success and is completely bad ass. This could be a custom Lamborghini, an elegant Jaguar, or a tough SUV. The choice is yours and boundless.

Now imagine you've won this new vehicle that you have always wanted in a contest. No strings attached, it's yours. At first, you're jumping up and down, absolutely ecstatic! It's always been a dream to own this vehicle, and now you have it! But after driving the vehicle for a few weeks, it no longer has the same allure it once did. It's also a pain to keep it clean, and you are constantly worried about someone scratching or dinging it. Soon you habituate back to the degree of happiness you had before you owned the vehicle. So even though you now have the item they've always wanted, your level of happiness regulates back to its original set point.

This is not dissimilar to a child with a new toy. They will initially fall in love with it, but eventually, they lose interest, and the toy is relegated to the toy bin with all the others that have been tossed aside.

The lesson is that buying something, no matter the expense, won't buy you happiness. It can cause temporary satiation, but not long lasting fulfillment. We as humans are always chasing that feeling of fulfillment; it is in our nature.

The cost of happiness? I've stated that the purchase of material goods cannot make you happy, but how much money does somebody need to make in a year to feel secure? How much does it cost to be happy? About $75,000 a year. A Princeton study in 2010 revealed that $75,000 was the magic yearly income to happiness. This is the point of separation on the Hedonic treadmill for most people. In other words, it is at this monetary set point that people are not stressed out financially. This allows them to shift their concerns to other areas of life. While $75,000 is an approximation that must be adjusted according to inflation, increased the cost of living, location, etc., it still demonstrates the point: once a person's income gets to the level where needing money is no longer an issue, they feel emotionally satiated and can, therefore, focus on other things.

More to the point, once they feel financially secure, they need to focus on things of actual importance; otherwise, boredom becomes a real possibility. This boredom is the first step on the Hedonic Treadmill. Boredom often manifests into distractions, and I've already spoken on the peril of distraction earlier. Boredom can also lead a person to lose respect for and fail to see the value in things they possess. This sets the Hedonic Treadmill into high gear.

No Respect

This shows that the journey to achieving financial success goes hand in hand with respecting that which you've achieved. The person you become in the process of

94

achieving a goal that you've work so hard to attain is much more important than the goal itself.

There are countless stories of people who win the lottery and then spend the money like water to buy any material thing they've ever wanted. They are still miserable and unfulfilled.

On the surface that doesn't even seem possible, but it comes back to the idea of having respect for a goal that is worthy of your time and effort, then ceaselessly putting in the work and effort to achieve it.

Putting in the energy and sacrifice to become a multi-millionaire builds not only a fortune but a person's resilience and self-esteem. There are many self-made millionaires who have lost everything financially only to come back stronger and more financially successful than before. The amount of money created is great but pales in comparison to the person who is created from this financial accomplishment. If you achieve everything you attempt with ease, then you aren't really testing yourself.

For example, becoming a black belt or instructor level in a Martial Art that you respect is impressive because no matter how rich you are, it can never be purchased monetarily. (Yes, I'm aware that there are some "Martial Arts" out there that will award you a black belt in a couple of years. These are not the arts of which I'm referring to.)

This skill level can never be gained simply because of the people you know, where you went to school or how much social celebrity you've reached. There is no shortcut. This goal takes time and can only be reached by consistent hard work and sacrifice.

The harder we have to work for something, the more it means to us. The greater the sacrifice, the more we value it. This is another reason why it's imperative to have Priorities that you genuinely love, respect, and desire. From this, your Purpose, Vision, and Primary Objectives will come from a place of purity and proper intent.

Chapter VII

Shark Bait

"You are more powerful than you know, act accordingly."

-Seth Godin-

My path to recovery continued to be a laborious and exacting one. Although my pace was slow, I was beginning to make legitimate improvements. After months of hard work, I was finally able to climb the three steps in the rehabilitation center with the help of my still compromised hands and arms stabilizing me. As trivial as that may sound, it felt like I'd summited Mt. Everest when I was able to have even that limited amount of compromised ambulation. As I stated before, the thing that motivated me wasn't pretty, but it was effective none the less. The thing that motivated me was fear.

Remember fear is like fire, a good servant but a horrible master, which is why you must learn to identify and control fear if you have any hopes of accomplishing your Primary Objectives.

The Hero and the Coward

"Iron" Mike Tyson was considered the hardest hitting Heavyweight in the history of Boxing. Tyson knocked out 26 of his first 28 professional opponents, 16 of those 26 in the first round. On June 27, 1988, Tyson knocked out Michael Spinks in 91 seconds of the first round to become the youngest undefeated, undisputed Heavyweight Boxing Champion in history. Often called "The Baddest Man on the Planet," Tyson was positively ferocious in the ring. He was said to "hit with bad intentions" and fought with an intensity few had seen in recent memory.

In light of these facts, it makes the following sentence that much more intriguing.

Many people are unaware that when Mike Tyson was an amateur boxer, he was literally so afraid before a match that he would cry before he would step into the ring. He had to be verbally coddled and corralled from the dressing room to walk into the arena. Tyson's mentor, father figure and trainer Constantine "Cus" D'Amato knew Tyson's trepidations were unwarranted. He knew that Tyson was well prepared for his opponent. He also knew a fighter's mind can be fragile before a fight. As D'Amato had said, "To see a man beaten not by a better opponent, but by himself is a tragedy." It was during one of these times of self-doubt that Cus told a young, frighten Mike Tyson a story to help ease his fears before a boxing match:

"What's the difference between a hero and a coward? The hero and the coward both feel the same thing, it's what they DO that makes them different. The hero feels the same amount of fear as the coward, but the hero uses his fear, projects it onto his opponent, while the coward runs. It's the same thing, fear, but it's what you do with it that matters."

With the motivation of this lesson fresh in his mind, Tyson would go into the ring and unleash hell on his opponent.

"Without fear, there can be no courage."

-Marcus Aurelius Anderson-

Cus D'Amato knew a fighter's mind could be fragile before a match. He had trained enough champions to know of this inevitability long before the fighter ever did. This is why he told the story of the Hero and the Coward early on in the fighter's development. The reality is that without fear, courage cannot reveal itself. It's easy to act courageously when there is no possibility of danger. That sort of false bravado is all too common. Courage is a feeling, but more importantly, it creates an action that can be committed only in the presence of legitimate fear. Courage without action isn't courage at all; it's only a coward's wish, and wishing doesn't get a damn thing done.

The fighter is honest. He is honest with himself about how he feels regarding the Adversity that he is about to face.

The fighter knows what he is capable. Because he knows of the damage he can inflict on his opponent, he understands the double-edged nature of violence. He realizes that if he can deal a devastating blow to his Adversary, one of equal strength can be dealt to him just as easily. The fighter knows that there is danger present because he represents the exacting danger his opponent sees before him. Because of the powerful effect of fear mixed with danger, the fighter must become accustomed to this presence in his body long before he steps in the ring. The adrenaline dump unleashed into the bloodstream will decimate a fighter ill-prepared for such an onslaught. A person of this unconditioned ilk will be defeated mentally before they even step foot on the canvas. The fighter has trained for months with the knowledge that on a date in the not so distant future, another fighter will await him in the arena. This Adversary will have had equal time and opportunity to train for their encounter, and he will offer no quarter in the square circle.

Every moment leading to the fight, there is a constant, ever increasing pressure growing. Every breath brings him closer to this approaching battle. The fighter, much like the soldier, knows of the hard work that needs to be done to succeed in battle. He couldn't forget about this Priority even if he tried.

Sleep will not necessarily come easily because of this, though the fighter's mind and body will be wary and fatigued from the necessary training. Some nights it will be impossible to find rest, while other mornings he will want nothing more than to sleep his days away from the fight. He will never walk into the arena without some sort of ache, pain, or injury. This is the nature of the beast when preparing for battle.

There are many levels of emotions when walking to the ring. Feeling the energy and excitement of the crowd as you approach adds another level of potential fear and anxiety. It is a feeling that few will experience and that words pale to describe. Imagine being in a car at the top of the steepest mountain you've ever encountered, then beginning to roll down the road realizing that there are no brakes. There will be family and friends in attendance. He will feel the additional pressure to impress and make them proud. What's more, he will also feel the fear of potential embarrassment. In addition to those well-wishers, there will be countless others who may hope to see the fighter fall. While it takes a team to craft a fighter, the fighter will ultimately step into battle alone. No one can assist him once the bell has rung, it is a task that only he can face.

The only thing between the fighter and his Adversary is fear, common sense, and air. The screaming crowd and bright lights can make our hero lose focus and begin to think about that which is of little importance regarding his imminent future. The fighter may begin questioning himself before the fight:

Could I have trained harder?

Did I train my technique enough?

Am I ready?

This is not the time the fighter should be asking these questions. That time has long since passed. Questioning any part of his preparation now does little to help him at the moment.

Cus D'Amato said, "When two men step into the ring, one and only one deserves to win. When you step into the ring, you gotta know you deserve to win. You gotta know destiny owes you victory, 'cause you trained harder than your opponent. You sparred harder. You ran farther." Before stepping into the ring, the fighter must let all of this anxiety go so that he can focus on the most important thing in the approaching moments.

What You Give

While in the highlands of the Dominican Republic on a Chiropractic mission trip, I learned a tremendous lesson. There had been violence in neighboring Haiti, the ripples of which were being felt on the Dominican side of the island. The church that was acting as our rendezvous point to get transportation throughout Puerto Plata was unable to find drivers due to the violence in the city, but they had an "alternate means" of transportation for a few of us who were more adventurous. I came to help as many people as I possibly could, so I was willing to accomplish this objective by any means possible.

The trek to the isolated village in the highlands was about an hour's ride...on horseback. It was overcast as we set out, but grew even darker as we increased in elevation. I could smell the precipitation and realized that we were probably going to get wet- mere moments before the initial downpour soaked us to the bone. The rain from the hills that drenched us was frigid, as some of the loud screams of surprise from those in our small group could attest to. I found the cloudburst positively invigorating and honestly couldn't help but smile during the storm.

As we rode on, the sound of the now gentle rainfall mixed with the rhythm of the horse's hoof beats produced a rather soothing cadence. The rain amplified the smell of the sugarcane growing along the trail, creating a positively majestic scene as the village came into view.

The village had about 50 inhabitants that came out to meet us. The first thing I heard as I dismounted was the sound of a baby crying. I asked the woman in Spanish how long the baby had been crying as I examined him still in his mother's arms. Even before she answered, I could tell it was a classic case of colic. I palpated the infant as the mother held him and found the vertebrae that were out of alignment. I gently adjusted the baby, who almost immediately stopped crying and promptly fell asleep.

The group that had gathered started murmuring then suddenly parted like the Red Sea as a very large man came walking towards the mother and child. He looked angrily at me and asked the woman what had happened to the baby. She told him what had transpired as he kept eyeing me, still unsure what to think. I realized as he took the child from the mother that this mountain of a man was the chief of the village and that I had adjusted his son. As he held the child and saw that it was not only safe but sleeping peacefully, he asked in Spanish: "How did you turn it off?" The whole village erupted in laughter as did he, slapping me hardily on the shoulder in thanks. I later learned this was the first time the baby had slept soundly in days and he was truly grateful. So grateful in fact that he killed his last chicken and cooked it for us. To go with the soon to be fried chicken, he had coffee brewed from coffee beans I saw picked before my very eyes. The fresh sugar cane sweetened this already delicious beverage beautifully. As I was drinking the delightful java, the sun even graced us with its presence.

Even though the village's offering may sound primitive, it is without a doubt one of the best meals I've ever had in my life. It was an amazing meal not just because it was fresh and delicious, but more importantly, because of what it represented. It showed that even though the people in the village had very little, they gave everything they were capable of to show their sincerest gratitude.

If two different people each gave you $100, logically you would think that they both gave you equal amounts of money. And monetarily speaking, they did. Let's say for the sake of argument that the first person is a multi-millionaire while the second person may have only had $100, all of which they have now given to you. So in reality, who gave you more? It's the same dollar amount, but the second person gave you everything that they had, and therein lies the lesson: It's not how much you possess that's important, it's how much you give that matters.

This is what the fighter must do when it is his time to fight. When the bell rings, the fighter must give everything that he has. He must not falter or hesitate; he must give it all. The hero shouldn't be concerned with how much energy he does or does not have, that is not of importance. What's important is that he gives every single ounce of that energy he possesses to give his best performance. If the fighter truly gives the best effort he can give in his moment of truth he will be victorious, regardless of whose arm is raised at the end of the fight. He must, therefore, focus all of his emotion and mental energy on making the next moments of his existence count. The fighter must trust that his movements will be smooth and powerful, that his reactions will be correct and precise and that his resolve will be worthy of the task before him. He must strip away that which is of ill importance, focusing only on what is his Priority. When all is said and done, all the fighter can do is focus on his Primary Objective. He has already crossed the Rubicon, the die has been cast, and he is now totally committed to this inevitability. He will not be able to control the outcome, ultimately that is out of his hands, but what he can control is how he acts while in the fray. What he can dictate is how hard he pushes himself against his Adversary. Ultimately, he must give all that he's got in the battle and forget about everything else that exists in the world in those moments. The rest of the world will still be there when he comes through the other side. This is the proving ground, this is his opportunity, and this is his time.

Adversity

After saying all of this about fear being born from to lack of preparation, how does this apply to Adversity? How can I possibly be prepared for every Adversity that I may face?

Well, you can't. The remedy that keeps us from resorting to the desperate use of the metaphorical "windmill technique" in other areas your life is through preventative preparation well before the possibility of the skills necessary. If you knew that there was a test that was going to be coming up that dictated how the rest of your life went, would you study for it? Would you study every spare moment you had, would you make time to prepare? Or would you be a person who just says: "I'm just going to wing it and see what happens?"

If you have an important test coming up like a driving test, finals in college or maybe even a test to get into your profession like a board or bar exam, I guarantee you will be preparing for it if you wanted to pass and do well on it.

This is what necessitates our need for Adversity. Many times a certain degree of Adversity is all that is required to bring out the best in us. That's why people always work more productively under a deadline. There is a reason why weight lifting is called resistance training. You're training yourself to resist. You're training yourself to resist against progressively more difficult Adversity, in this case, that physical Adversity is a heavier weight, and the only way to get stronger is to progressively learn to overcome and master more and more Adversity. It is through this type of training that we are able to bring that mental strength and resolve into other realms of our lives and development, and like lifting weights, there will be a time when you simply cannot lift the burden placed upon you. If you can't, it's ok to rest and catch your breath, but you'll never gain any actual strength if you let your resting turn into capitulation. So go out and actively seek the Adversity that you wish to overcome, the greater the better. It is only through mastering these hardships that we can hope to gain the strength required to achieve our other greater goals.

People have all kinds of excuses that they call "reasons." But all I hear when they give these well-crafted "reasons" is, "my happiness isn't worth sacrificing the life I have currently." These are just semantics for things that they will never achieve.

When a person claims to want to change their life but then doesn't act on it, it's not because they are happy with their current situation. It's because they are complacent. It's because they are lazy and their new life isn't worth even the slightest inconvenience. Honestly, if you aren't happy with your life then what have you got to lose? If you're afraid to lose mediocrity, then you'll be too afraid to embrace greatness while in its presence. You have nothing to lose and everything to gain. I for one would rather die of thirst than drink from the cup of mediocrity again.

There is a mental misconception that by having an excuse, it somehow puts the issue on hold as if they've pushed pause. This allows the person more mental preoccupation that acts as a stylized form of distraction and pacification, but while they've stopped thinking about actually improving their life, time marches on. So even though you may not want to deal with the issue at hand, it will continue to grow and take its course, with or without you.

Fear

"Nothing breeds confidence like preparation."

-Marcus Aurelius Anderson-

Fear gets a bum rap because people always assume the worst in the face of this potential. Fear, like Adversity, is an opportunity with high-stakes. Nothing breeds confidence like focused preparation; nothing builds conviction like purposeful action.

When emotions run high, it's sometimes difficult to know exactly what it is we are feeling. Often times we are experiencing not one, but several emotions at once, which can leave us feeling uncertain and confused among other things.

Before anything from a first date to an inevitable and uncomfortable conversation you are dreading, there are many emotions at play. We can feel equally nauseated from the feelings of fear, excitement, seasickness, or just bad tacos.

Fear and excitement are two emotions that can create similar feelings, and they often stem from the same stimulus.

Before I step on stage to give a talk, I have both of these emotions pumping through my veins to varying degrees. But it is my preparation beforehand that dictates which of these I experience the greatest degree of before I begin to speak.

If I didn't have a speech prepared and had no idea what I was going to say before I went on stage, then the primary emotion I would feel may be fear and anxiety. In this case, much like the case of the fighter who is ill-prepared, the resulting adrenaline rush may very well impede my ability to give a clear, well- thought out and concise presentation. However, if I am well polished and practiced before my professional speaking engagement, I will still feel both fear and excitement. In this case, it will be a much greater degree of excitement than fear or anxiety. Remember that adrenaline is released in response to a perceived fight-or-flight situation, and if we aren't properly prepared, then many things can seem like a threat. This causes an increase in heart rate, an increase in blood sugar levels and pupil dilatation. All of these physiological responses are ways the body prepares itself for the potential of physical combat. But while adrenaline temporarily increases the physical abilities of the body (increased strength, decreased pain levels, etc.) it simultaneously decreases cognitive and fine motor skills (higher thinking, dexterous hand capacities, etc.).

This explains the grotesque body motions and the all too common "windmill technique" seen when an untrained person gets into a physical altercation. The adrenaline dump takes over and all the body can do is swing wildly in hopes of connecting with their opponent. This demonstrates the necessity to differentiate between these two powerful emotions. If one is confused with the other, the end results can be tragic.

For example, imagine something you're scared of. Think of the emotions that come to you. Now, think of something you're really excited about. Examine your feelings regarding this as well. You will notice similarities in the thoughts, feelings, and reactions regarding these two scenarios. They both make your pulse race and give you butterflies in your stomach. You must ask yourself: are you feeling excitement disguised as fear? Or are you genuinely afraid because you are ill-prepared for what's about to occur? This is your litmus test—If you're scared, you're unprepared. If you're prepared, though you may be afraid, your excitement outweighs your fear.

I realize that this is a skill that takes time to develop. And the only way to hone a skill is through consistent repetition. I also understand that we can't be ready for every potential situation, it is impossible. However, by employing the 80/20 principle, it allows you to be prepared in a few key areas that will give you confidence in the vast majority of situations you will run into from day to day. This mindset of confidence from preparation will then bleed over into to other areas of life as well.

This is why people who have studied martial arts for any appreciable amount of time have developed a quiet confidence. They know that at the lowest human common denominator if a verbal disagreement they are involved in comes to blows, they can protect themselves. Therefore, intimidation and veiled threats do not create the same kind of influence on them the way they would a person who is insecure and unprepared.

This confidence can be recognized in their voice, eye contact, and body language regarding any situation. It is the characteristic that separates the posture of predator and prey; and, because of this innate knowledge, everyone wants to appear confident even when they are not. In some, this causes overcompensation both verbally and physically. A person who lacks confidence but wants to appear so will exhibit their perception of confidence, this imitation of confidence often manifests itself as arrogance.

Swagger In, Stagger Out

Ever since I was a child, Martial Arts have been a big part of my life. The lessons learned and discipline it instilled in me has helped in every facet of my life.

The Martial Arts attract many different kinds of people. Some begin training strictly to learn self-defense, but others will come in search of more than that. Many train to develop greater self-confidence. Others come to get stronger, improve cardiovascular fitness, develop better mental focus, in addition having an exciting workout in the process. The overwhelming majority of people don't start training with the intention of ever stepping into the ring or the cage to fight professionally, but there are a few that don't want to learn- they simply want to try test themselves or worse, to try to beat other people up. If they have physical characteristics that give them an immediate advantage such as size and strength, they will rely on these things immediately. They will come to rely on their natural attributes until those abilities take them as far as it can. These practitioners that are natural athletes may do well in the beginning. Some can learn a tremendous amount very quickly.

The Achilles' heel of these gifted athletes is the fact that they are indeed so talented and that things normally come to them rather easily, and because of this proclivity for learning things easily, whenever they are put under any actual pressure, they fall apart at the seams when they are truly tested.

Oftentimes the people with the most athletic ability are the first to quit when they are faced with any legitimate Adversity. They aren't used to being pressed to improve because they are usually the ones who are pushing the pace. Once they go against a person who is better than they are, this is when the actual learning begins. This is when they must disengage their ego in order to be humble enough to learn and improve. For some, this is not the case. They will come back long enough to simply test their metal and once they've been bested enough times, many will quit training altogether. Now the person who essentially wanted to come in to bully others is now being bullied, and they don't like it one bit. They can dish it out but often can't take it. I find it intriguing that the very thing that attracted them to enter this place, their romantic notion regarding violence and danger, is what they now fear. Talent is given, but greatness is something that must be earned, and again, it is Adversity that is needed to create greatness.

The Martial Artist who has had to work hard for everything from the very beginning of their training retains his composure and exhibits grace under pressure because nothing has come easily for them—all of their lessons have been well learned and earned. They have already questioned their own heart and spirit a thousand times before they will be tested by any Adversary. They've questioned himself every time they performed a technique and every time they went to train, and this has given them tremendous resilience. They have shown the heart and drive to go back to try to get better, even when they seemed to be getting little to no results.

I knew an international level competitor who was very good and accustomed to winning. They dominated at a local and national level in every event that they entered. When they were eventually beat by a person that was better than they were, they understood the lesson—they realize that they learned much more from a loss then they do from any victory. This loss subsequently reshaped the competitor's mentality, goals, and conditioning program.

While the sting of a loss hurts at the time, it can be one of the best things that could happen to you. It shows you the glaring weaknesses in your approach. You can only coach a person to improve on the weaknesses and flaws of their technique for so long. Their shortcomings become apparent when an Adversary shines a light on these facts so glaringly that it is impossible to deny.

One of the best ways to improve is to seek out those better and more skill than you are, this forces you to compete at a higher level and accelerates the learning curve tremendously.

It's a necessity to seek out and embrace Adversity to progress faster. In martial arts, one of the best ways to improve is to train and spar with people that are better than you. This forces you to perform at a higher level and accelerates the learning curve tremendously, though it can be daunting at first. There will be times when you don't want to go to class to train, but it's imperative that on days like that, you force yourself to go. Pain and discomfort are the best teachers. It is during these times of self-imposed Adversity that you learn the most not only about your skillset but about yourself as well. Going back to class after class and having your ego put in check every time, is one of the best ways to build mental fortitude and resilience for the real world. Does this mean that you must go back and get beaten up and bloodied every time you train? Absolutely not, though if you have a fight coming up, the blood and sweat are part of the price for greatness.

If you are a recreational trainer this doesn't mean that you have to get "beat up" per se, but doing drills and training with a more skilled person helps you notice the differences in your technique and theirs. Their timing, sensitivity, and fluidity will be better than your own. This kind of training will help bring out the best in you as a Martial Artist and as inspire you to reach a higher skill level.

This models the idea that you are the average of the five people you spend the most time with. This goes not for just social and financial situations, but for martial arts training as well. If you train with lions, you have no choice but to become one.

Like most things in life, ultimately it is your decision on how hard you push yourself. If you are the smartest person in the room, then find another room, preferably with smarter people than yourself. If you are bored in your competitions, then find tougher competition, or find a way to limit your skill set to make your opponent more difficult to beat.

Brazilian Jiu-Jitsu legend Rickson Gracie would often put one hand in his belt, making him essentially a one-armed fighter. This limitation on his part made his training partner artificially better and more difficult to fight than if Gracie were able to use his full physical faculties and capacities. Learning to fight with literally one arm behind his back improved his skills while allowing his opponent a better chance to learn as well.

The discipline of mindset from the Martial Arts also pays dividends in the other areas of your life. It teaches you to keep an enduring work ethic that doesn't let you give up on yourself when life kicks you in the teeth. It helps you know that no matter how bad your day was at work, that you've endured far worse and will continue to willingly, regardless of how many times you get hit or submitted. Accept it for what it is and be happy with the lesson. When you look back, you'll see that it wasn't as bad as you thought it was at the time. You'll also find the wisdom and self-knowledge you learned was well worth the price of the Adversity you faced.

Loser

Here's the reality: It's actually a bad thing NOT to lose. Imagine a child who was always allowed to win at whatever game they played. While letting them win initially is good, it's more important to teach them to lose, to learn and remain humble. If this child was allowed to win up until they become a teenager, imagine what a spoiled brat they would be. They would exhibit the traits that come with the cocky arrogance of their unbeatable self-perception: uncoachable, disrespectful, selfish, and undisciplined to name a few.

Now think of the situation when they are beaten for the first time. Imagine the epic meltdown that would ensue. We see this today in adults who practically have a full-on temper tantrum because they are so accustomed to getting everything they want. This is a horrible thing to see. If it's not a temper tantrum, it may be something far worse for the individual. If they have been coddled and given everything without earning it from day one, when they go out into the real world, they learn that it pulls punches for no one.

"In nature, there are neither rewards nor punishments; there are consequences."

-Robert Green Ingersoll-

If a person isn't prepared for the consequences of reality, it can crush their confidence and self-esteem. This is a sad situation, especially when you consider that it could've been easily prevented if they had learned the lesson of humility at a young age.

"When it feels like you're a move behind in a fight, you're not...you're actually two or three."

-Sifu LaDell Elliott-

Remember that failure is a necessity of learning. When you first start the martial arts, you never do any technique perfectly. The first time you spar you will most likely not beat an opponent decisively or submit them soundly, nor should you attempt to.

In the same way that we want to embrace the success of achievement, we should understand that we need to accept the reality of failure twice as strongly because it is the failure that helps us find the path to success.

I've seen countless beginners get frustrated when sparring or rolling (sparring or wrestling in Jiu-Jitsu). It's easy to mentally beat yourself, especially when you feel like an opponent is "winning." Often there is a mental gap and reactive thought process: "Damn it, that's the third time they've scored on me! This sucks!" While all these thoughts are going through the white belts mind, it clouds their present thought process. This consequently sets them up for failure when attempting to respond to the next move of your opponent.

1. Realize that this is not a fight.

This a game, its play. To see it as such will take the pressure off of you. Removing the stakes of victory and defeat allows a more relaxed learning environment. The fight happens outside of the academy, and this is how you prepare for it.

The idea is to gain experience, not victory. Victory will come in the future, after more experience, and experience is what you're gathering now, from "losing" in your mind.

Even if you get submitted 100 times, it just means you're learning. A person taps thousands of times on the road to black belt; and even then, there are high-level black belts that still tap every day in training. This doesn't mean that they aren't good black belts; on the contrary, this means they willingly put themselves in difficult positions in order to learn more.

This means that they leave their ego out of their training because they know that ego will slow a person's progress more than any other Adversary you will ever face.

Believe me, nobody goes to work the next day and tells all their co-workers how they "tapped out the new guy" who consequently, had absolutely no prior experience.

2. 'Don't focus on what just happened, focus on what's happening now. This lets you see opportunities to make things happen later. Don't hold on to the mistake. Release it, learn from it, and move on. If you do not, you'll be many moves behind in the encounter, which usually means you'll be "beaten" soon enough.

3. You'll make mistakes. If you're not, then you're not asking enough of yourself. In life, you will make mistakes, period. Don't wallow and focus on the negative, just dust yourself off and try to accentuate the positive to move forward. The first time anyone rolls/spars with a higher-level person, and that means anyone who has more than a few months experience than you do, you will get defeated. You may get angry or even discouraged. But why? You must

realize that anyone who is successful now has had to begin in the same place you are standing now, and this goes for anything from martial arts to business and entrepreneurship. Have you been good at everything you've ever tried the first time? Has everything you've ever done in your life come quickly, naturally and easily?

For your sake, I certainly hope it hasn't. If everything you have ever tried came easily and without effort, then you must be the most naturally gifted person in the history of mankind. And if it has, then I truly feel sorry for you. I hope you've had to face at least some form of Adversity; otherwise, you're going to be in for a very rude awakening in life when you eventually do fail at something. Ask yourself what exactly are you afraid of? Are you afraid of learning where your weaknesses lie? Because if you are, this is called ego- and ego can get you killed.

Death by Ego

The savage beauty of South Africa in the summer is positively breathtaking. That morning as we set out in the choppy waters where the Indian and the Atlantic Ocean converged around the Cape of Good Hope, I was excited about the possibilities the day held. The 32-foot fishing boat fought through the rough sea as we headed south for a day of deep sea fishing. The last few weeks in South Africa had been one amazing experience after another, and today would prove to be especially exciting.

Originally from the Midwest, I didn't grow up around the ocean. Spending time on the East and West coast helped me discover the captivating nature of the ocean's splendor and power, but even during those times, I'd never taken the opportunity to go deep sea fishing before.

As we continued out of sight of land, the ocean grew choppier, and the waves grew ever larger. Being on the boat with friends and family made the entire experience more enjoyable, but when the boat stopped, the waves seemed to throw our boat up and down all the more. I had taken medication for motion sickness before we left just in case, but it didn't seem to be working. It hit me rather quickly that I hadn't had enough time to get acclimated and develop my "sea legs." Evidently, it was written all over my face because right about then, the captain of the boat announced in his thick South African accent:

"Ok people, if ANYBODY is feeling sick, as in you're going to THROW UP, do it near the side of the boat. Lie down ON YOUR SIDE and curl up next to the railing in the fetal position, but whatever you do, DO NOT STAND UP AND THROW UP!"

He looked at me during the most emphatic portion of his announcement, so I must have looked green in the face by now. My stomach was as sloshy as the ocean at this point. It was not a question of "if" but "when" I was going to throw up. About that time someone in the crew yells out, "Look, off of the starboard side, seals 20 meters!" As everyone turned to look, I realized that this was my opportunity to "yell groceries" over the port side of the vessel without everyone seeing me.

There is a huge correlation between seals and sharks in the giant ecosystem that is the ocean. In hindsight, this was the knowledge that I had, but it was not exactly a priority as I went to go throw up unceremoniously over the side of the boat on the choppy sea.

I leaned over the edge as best I could, holding onto the railing for dear life. As I interlocked my arms around the bar of the railing, I proceeded to "chum" to use the nautical term. Immediately, I heard the crowd on the other side of the boat erupt into cheers and screams of surprise and excitement. Oh, fantastic. That's just wonderful, here I am miserably seasick, and all my friends and family can do is laugh and make fun of me. Well, it is what it is. There's little I can do at this point; maybe it'll make for a funny and memorable story for later.

In between waves of sickness, I turned to face the inevitable music of them laughing and pointing at me. I'm sure a cell phone camera or two would be rolling to document my disgrace. How embarrassing. But when I turned around, no one was looking at me at all. Not a soul had seen my disgraceful display. They were all still staring transfixed on the starboard side. Really? How interesting could a bunch of seals be anyway? As I was able to peer between them from my vantage point, I caught a glimpse of what had caused this uproar. I could make out the shapes of the seals swimming in a single file formation on the surface of the water when seemingly out of nowhere, there was a huge explosion. It was a Great White. This monster hit a seal with such velocity as it breached the surface that it sent the tiny mammal sailing 15 feet in the air from the impact. For the first time in an hour, I stopped feeling seasick. I felt even worse.

Unable to process what I had just seen, I immediately turned back to my perch to continue my previous activity. Only this time, nothing happened. I thought that getting seasick while out in the middle of the ocean, surrounded by breaching Great White sharks was one of the worst things that could happen to anybody. I was sorely mistaken.

What is worse is to be dry heaving uncontrollably over the side of the boat while out in the middle of the ocean, surrounded by breaching Great White sharks. It was like something out of a bad movie, and that's exactly what was happening to me.

118

When you are dry heaving, it is even more violent than getting sick, because your entire body tries to help expel your stomach contents, even though there is none to offer at this point. Unfortunately, that also means that all the muscles in your body begin to contract violently with each wave of nausea. In this case, holding onto the railing will do little to help you. As I stood up holding onto the railing, my body violently heaved, and my legs kicked out and contracted suddenly. I could feel my body involuntarily jumping overboard as I held on for dear life. The last thing I saw over the port side as I began to go overboard was the giant silhouette of a shark with its menacing dorsal fin seeming to track my movement. "Well, this is it. This is how I die. Death by ego." At the last possible moment and still dangling from the railing, I was pulled back onboard by the captain and crew. My feet had touched the ocean surface, but miraculously I was unscathed. Oh, so THAT'S why the captain said not to stand up if you were going to be sick.

The lesson:

My ego and pride had nearly gotten me killed. I was more concerned with saving face in front of other people then I was taking the captain's advice, I had nearly lost much more than just my face, as it were. I had been more concerned with being embarrassed than I was with my safety. Because of my stupid pride, I was more fearful of the opinions of others than I was of a Great White shark. In hindsight, I now see how incredibly dumb that sounds. See how incredibly dumb that sounds?

Stop Fearing What Others Think

"There is only one way to avoid criticism: do nothing, say nothing, and be nothing."

-Aristotle-

Everyone is afraid of failing. They fear to attempt the things they want because they fear failure. They believe that "failure "means the end of achieving that goal or ambition. Honestly, nothing could be further from the truth. Failure is a requirement for success.

To succeed, we must first try and often fail to see where improvements are needed. Like the Martial Arts competitor, we learn 100X more from a defeat then we do from a victory. Victory has an intoxicating effect, and this can prove to be more detrimental than any loss. Winning often teaches you little and will sometimes encourage even the worst habits if they just so happened to prove successful in this specific encounter.

A loss shows you the glaring weaknesses that need to be improved upon, so don't fear failure, because the fear of failure can stop success dead in its tracks. A mistake is simply an investment in the future. Seek out failure; it is part of the process.

Failure isn't the end of an endeavor; it's just the beginning. Failure simply makes you question how much you want your goal. That's one of the great things about fear; it makes you question yourself and your motives constantly. This forces one to continually reinforce your actions by having a target in mind. Having this unrelenting drive is what makes us find other ways to succeed. You must learn to embrace the uncertainty, to be able to co-exist with it. You must learn to be tolerant a certain degree of fear because it doesn't go away. Learn to dance with the fear and the risk. Because if what you want is worth having, then the fear never goes away entirely. There will always be a sliver of it floating in your subconscious, so if you truly want something, you'll have to learn to do it afraid.

People are afraid to lose for many reasons. But the biggest, yet most unimportant reason, is that they worry what others will think. This is often what stops people from even attempting the things they've always wanted to try. How do you remedy this? The key is not to care what others think. Ever. I can think of no sadder reason for a person to not follow their dreams than fearing the opinions of others.

"When you're 20 you care what everyone thinks, when you're 40 you stop caring what everyone thinks, when you're 60 you realize no one was ever thinking about you in the first place. Do you have enemies? Good. That means you've stood up for something, sometime in your life."

-Winston Churchill-

The reason I go into detail about what constitutes genuine fear is that most of the things people are labeling as fear are nowhere close fear at all. Most of us are in no immediate physical danger like the fighter or soldier. For many of us, there is little actual danger to be faced from day to day. This means we are out of touch with real fear and instead, project it onto things that do not merit it. We perceive what a person says or thinks to be dangerous. We get mad at the person who is driving too slow or doesn't use their turn signal when in the grand scheme of things, this means nothing. The release of adrenalin is therefore often misplaced. We are repeatedly releasing the chemical over and over throughout the day causing a constant state of aggravation, agitation, and anxiety.

What people are calling fear is simply their over concern regarding the opinions of others. Unfortunately, in many ways, this is even more detrimental than any legitimate fear could ever be.

Instinctually as humans, we still have the tribal mentality. We want to be accepted by others. Our ancestors understood that banding together allowed the sharing of resources, knowledge, and manpower. This proved advantageous regarding hunting, building and tribal security against outside threats as well. This culture was much easier than trying to survive alone, but what many don't realize is that it's natural to not fit in with those around them. It's okay to not have the same thoughts, desires, and beliefs as those around you. Initially, the people who you are surrounded by have much more to do with proximity than compatibility. This fact alone is your indication that you should continue pursuing your goals because following this path will lead you to cross paths with those who are more like you. Your ceaseless desire to improve and better yourself will cause some around you to feel uncomfortable, possibly because they are not as motivated or disciplined as you are. These people will doubt you and maybe even gossip about you. This is yet another subtle form of Adversity. No matter, use your haters as motivators.

Hard work creates self-belief, and eventually you come to a point where you are confident enough to not care about what others think. You evolve to the understanding that those whose opinions you most cared about, then later came to ignore, were irrelevant, to begin with. Therefore, the lesson that should be exercised from the very beginning is to pursue your dreams and goals relentlessly, because nobody is paying attention either way. You will come to find the people whose opinion you were most concerned with weren't even paying attention to your victories or defeats.

I realize now that before my injury, I feared the opinions of others. At the time, I honestly didn't think I did. But in hindsight, I now see that some of my previous hesitations were based on my fear of the opinions of others. I no longer have that issue. After the realization that I'd feared others opinion more than I valued my own, I became fearless. This is my life. My time is limited and therefore, all the more precious. And so is yours. I now live life on my terms. I don't allow myself the luxury of caring what people may or may not think of me. Yes, I maintain awareness of such things to an extent, but I now take everything with a grain of salt to keep myself honest.

Concerning yourself with what others think includes being concerned with what close friends and family will think, and for some, this will be the hardest truth to accept. If you don't care about someone else's opinion, you will act in a way that is uninhibited. Most are not doing that at all. They act as if they are simply trying to do something without getting caught. This in and of itself is an intellectual act of cowardice. Yet through all of this, many never realize that they could follow their dreams and be led by their ambitions too. They don't realize this because failing in the limelight of the opinion of others is what they fear most. They are afraid to fail, in any way, shape or form.

Why do we concern ourselves so much with the thoughts of people we don't even know? Why does the opinion of a person, whose opinion we may not even care for or respect if we got to know in person, stifle us into living our lives in such a meek manner?

As a society, we simultaneously worship and hate the people that have the courage and ambition to go out and follow their dreams, but revel and cheer inwardly and possibly outwardly when they stumble and fall. Are you fearful of the opinions of others because you are afraid that what they say will be somehow correct? If so, it is because you aren't yet comfortable with yourself in your skin, and this is where self-knowledge becomes indispensable.

Just because someone calls you a giant, pink giraffe does not make it so. By knowing thyself, you understand the statement is baseless and untrue. To be yourself means you can stand comfortably in your truth and self-knowledge. The reality is that no matter what you do, there will be someone who will not like, agree or simply be jealous of you in some capacity. Not everyone is going to like me, and that's fine.

Take pizza for example. Who doesn't like pizza right? Now realize that there are tens of thousands who positively hate pizza. Does that make the pizza you love bad or unworthy in some manner? Of course not. It's called personal preference. Would it do any good to try to change the opinions of those who don't like pizza? Probably not. Should pizza suddenly try to change itself into something that is more palatable to those who don't like it in the first place? Again, no. To change pizza would turn it into something that I and countless others no longer like as much. In the end, by trying to make everyone like it, pizza becomes less liked in the long run.

This would be similar to responding to every single opinion you disagree with on social media. I have neither the time nor the inclination for such a thing. The time I have is far too precious to spend on something that is, at best, a huge exercise in futility, and honestly, even if you had the desire to go through point-by-point and explain why you disagree with someone's opinion, more than likely it would change little to do so because the other person already has a made-up mind. All it takes for anyone to voice their opinion today is a Wi-Fi connection; and while this may make many feel entitled, few are qualified to have an opinion about many of the things of which they are criticizing. Understand that the people who throw drive-by insults don't care about you either. You must realize that the people who are casting stones at you are more than likely doing the same to countless other people as well. This means that they don't care about you beyond the fact that they want to express their opinion and then move on. Don't let people project their shortcoming or limitations on you. Honestly, it makes no sense to give their opinions a second thought. Stop caring what they think because the only person whose opinion you should care about should be your own. Because at the end of the day, those who spit the most venom don't give you a second thought either.

Having the ability to do what you want to do without even taking the opinions of others into consideration is true freedom. You are untethered and able to express yourself freely without inhibition. This is the kind of freedom that lets one reach their highest potential. It grants the liberation to make groundbreaking ideas and breakthroughs that can change not only their own life but potentially the lives of millions.

Motivation

"We know nothing about motivation, all we can do is write books about it."

-Peter Drucker-

Ah yes, motivation, the intellectual porn that everyone salivates about. A person that watches a motivating video clip reveals something about them. It tells that they are unmotivated enough to realize that they need motivation. The thing people want the most from motivation cannot be found in a soundbite or inspirational quote. It takes time, effort, dedication, and most of all, consistency to reach the levels of continued motivation that they desire most. The very reason why so many people love soundbites and inspirational quotes is because it is the motivational equivalent of junk food.

When dissected we see that to the majority, motivation is a feeling or emotion. People love reading things that motivate them, because it makes them feel good, at least for a little while. The emotion of motivation is short lived.

Which is why by February, most have already abandoned their once all too precious New Year's Resolutions. Enthusiasm and inspiration always come in waves. This is why it is imperative to attack your goal in the beginning as much as possible. We will go much further into these steps in the next chapter.

While I hope my story motivates and inspires you, I'm not here to motivate you. I don't need to motivate you because you are already motivated, and because you are already motivated, you must look within yourself to find what that motivation is, and no, I don't mean that in some weird, esoteric, fortune cookie kind of way either.

External stimuli can cause motivation for the moment, but actual motivation comes from within. The external stimuli are the spark, but you must build the fire. The spark I make takes but an instant, it's building the fire that takes the longest.

Motivational speakers are fun to watch but let's be honest, in actuality, they don't do anything. Yes, they make you feel inspired and motivated for a few moments, but these are feelings that are transient. They are a cheerleader for your emotions, and of course, everybody likes that.

Motivational speakers can't motivate you to do something that you're not already motivated internally to do in some capacity. Does a motivational speaker have to motivate you to sleep? Do you need to be motivated to eat? How about to have sex? Of course not, because these are needs. There's something within all of us that we want to accomplish that is a "need" as well, and it's up to you to uncover what that is—which is exactly why we spent so much time in the previous chapters finding what those needs represent to you.

Asking someone else to keep you motivated 24/7 would be like hiring a trainer to help you get into shape, except you aren't the one doing the workout, the trainer does. While watching the trainer work out may be "motivating," in the end, it does little to help transform your body and mind for the better.

Another example would be if I were thirsty on a hot summer's day. If I'm incredibly parched and my favorite cold, refreshing beverage is within my grasp, it will still do nothing to quench my thirst. I can whine and complain about how thirsty I am all I want, but it will not satiate me. Even if another person comes over because of my lamenting, they cannot drink the beverage for me. I must put forth the effort to pick it up and consume it myself to receive the benefits of it. Even if another holds the glass for me, it is up to me to drink it in. These things that you want so badly in your life are things that only you can do for yourself and have it mean what it should to you. With all that said, a person can do incredible things when they find actual motivation.

Actual Motivation

Some people are confused as to what motivation legitimately is. Many will use the words motivation, inspiration, and enthusiasm interchangeably. While these words are similar, this does not mean they are necessarily equivalent. I want to clarify what I consider to be motivation, at least for the sake of this discussion. Let's find a "motivational" subject to discuss: Rent.

When rent is due at the first of the month, I am not "inspired" nor do I have a tremendous amount of "enthusiasm" to pay it, but I am motivated to do so none the less. I am motivated to pay rent, not for the sake of paying it, instead, I am motivated by the potential alternative that would occur if I were not to pay in a timely fashion. I don't like the idea of paying a late fee, taking a hit on my credit score or worse, being kicked out of my home. These would be some of the alternatives to not paying rent. As we can see, motivation, though like inspiration and enthusiasm, is a very different thing indeed.

It is said that some of the best motivators in life are the pursuit of pleasure and the avoidance of pain. I would tend to agree with that statement for the most part. I have found in my experience that mental and physical fatigue are some of the most common obstacles that people have regarding motivation. This is why we will use it in the following example to show The 5 Levels of Motivation.

When a man is very tired, think of these possible scenarios:

Level 1. He's given an opportunity of having dinner and drinks with friends without any other responsibilities. Though tired, he will still go.

Level 2. He's given the opportunity to spend time with a woman that he finds incredibly attractive. He will push through fatigue to do this as well.

These first two levels show how far we can push when we are in a pleasure-seeking mode, again we can push through fatigue for something we find desirable as a form of motivation. The next few examples represent a higher level of motivation. He's in the same level of fatigue as above:

Level 3. If he's tired but feels that he is in physical danger, a physical threat for example, then the mind can will the body to press on beyond his fatigue.

Level 4. He's dead tired but someone he holds dear is in danger. If his wife, kids, family member, or close friends were in danger, again he would somehow find the strength to press through.

These are examples of avoidance of pain or danger mode.

The 5th level is the highest because it transcends pleasure seeking, avoidance of pain/danger and more.

In addition to the first 4 Levels think, of any physical or mental ability you possess now that you most cherish. This could be anything from a physical skill to intellectual abilities and emotional capacities.

Level 5. He's exhausted but:

He realizes that this may be his last opportunity to achieve that which he truly wants. This represents his only chance of ever being capable of actualizing his potential. This is the level of motivation a prisoner has to escape prison. This is the level of motivation a soldier has when he fights his Adversary to protect his homeland, family, and way of life. This is the level of motivation I attained during my injury and subsequent recovery. This is the level of motivation needed for you to achieve your biggest goals, hopes, and desires. This is the level of motivation you should aspire to uncover within yourself because every choice you make from here on out involves a varying degree of all 5 Levels now that you've become aware of them.

What this demonstrates is that there are boundless levels of this strength, resolve, and resilience designed to mirror whatever Adversity we are brave enough to face. Like Parkinson's Law (work expands to fill the time available for its completion) our strength, resolve, and resilience are forced to expand in response to the level of Adversity we are attempting to overcome.

There are still as of yet, untouched supplies of all of these things and even more within every one of us. We never knew these things existed because we have never pushed ourselves far enough to discover them. The thing that drives us to act in this manner is what I would consider actual motivation. Level 5 is the level that should be engaged when attacking your Primary Objectives.

I understand that there will be times when we feel so fatigued that we don't want to go on. When you get to this point, just remind yourself that when your goals and dream are actualized, the fatigue you felt getting there will be long forgotten.

"The Human tendency is to look for an easy way of doing things. People put in a lot of time and effort into looking for shortcuts. It's not that hard to outwork an opponent. Because most people don't know how to push themselves to their true potential."

-Dan Gable, 1972 Olympic Gold Medalist-

We must push ourselves to our boundaries and beyond to know what we are truly capable of. When this is done consistently, we soon realize that the first boundary we encountered was our own self-imposed mental limitation. Then eventually as we gain more experience and get even stronger, we come to realize that every limitation we face is our own self-imposed limitation. There are no limits or boundaries except for the ones that we artificially manufacture.

The point is we all have huge amounts of resolve, strength, and ferocious intelligence that we never even get close to bringing to full bare. This dictates that if we can tap into even a small percentage of this reserve, we could do even greater things than what we are currently asking ourselves at this very moment. Motivation is something that we all have within us. Once you uncover your motivation, there's little that can be done to stop you. If you choose not to discover your own motivation that you already possess, then there's nothing that I or anybody else can do to help you; and ultimately, this is a decision that only you can make for yourself.

Chapter VIII

Say Uncle

"I will either find a way or make one."

-Hannibal-

Though I was slowly regaining some of my ability to walk, I was still trepidatious about my recovery. While the numbness in my extremities was unrelenting, I continued to take one day at a time trying to recover to the best of my abilities.

My future and recovery were far from certain. I could stall or even regress in my improvement at any moment, so I was doing everything in my power to continue making strides. During one of my physical therapy sessions, my therapist was looking at my pre-operation MRI for the first time. He asked me what a normal day of activity was like for me. He then inquired about the symptomatology I exhibited before I was unable to move.

I told him about the usual training that was required in the infantry, and that I'd had varying degrees of these symptoms for the last six months give or take.

He looked at the MRI in silence for a few more moments before he finally spoke. "I just don't understand it," he said still staring in disbelief at my MRI. "You shouldn't have even been physically able to walk, let alone run and carry heavy weight for miles at a time. Your body should have given out LONG before you were rushed to the hospital. How were you able to do all that crazy stuff in your condition!?"

I sat in silence because I truly had no answer either. Finally, after a few moments, I replied, "I honestly don't know, I guess my mind was just stronger than my body."

There is strength, and then there is will. Will is what gets you through when your strength abandons you. This is a testament to the strength of the human mind. My body literally should not have been able to do all the intense training that I'd been doing for the last several months. Because my mind willed it, I was able to press my compromised body on further than it should've ever been able to go.

I can think of no better example of how vitally important and truly powerful one's mindset can be. It never occurred to me that there was any physical reason that I shouldn't be able to achieve my objectives, and because I never allowed it to enter my realm of possibility mentally, I left myself no other choice but to overcome these self-perceived "weaknesses" I was experiencing. I could push my body to the breaking point and beyond, because of one thing: Belief.

I legitimately believed it to be true that I could do these things. These were things I was confident I could do. In my mind, I could think of no reason that I shouldn't be able to meet the challenges set before me.

Know Faith, No Fear

Faith and fear both ask you to believe in something that you cannot see. When put into a situation we are uncertain of our mind fills in the blanks to create a complete picture. Consequently, we end up believing whichever of these two options we happen to believe in most strongly at the time.

Fear is usually the easiest to believe in because it takes very little effort to be afraid regarding a situation we are already uncertain of. Conversely, belief can require a tremendous effort to create, even in the smallest amounts, regarding a situation in which we are already apprehensive. Therefore, if you want to have even a hope of succeeding, you must not put your faith in fear. You MUST put your faith in yourself and believe in your abilities.

Yes, yes, I know. You've heard this all before. Yes, I understand that that sounds powerful but vague and nonspecific. Just hear me out. It is indeed much easier said than done, especially if the Adversity you face is particularly daunting, that's why I'm going to give you the secret developing genuine belief in yourself, even when you feel that there is no chance of succeeding.

The secret is this: you don't have to succeed the first time you attempt anything. You must understand that you will likely have to attempt something multiple times to gain that which you truly desire.

"The first draft of everything is shit."

-Ernest Hemingway-

Failing the first time at anything is to be expected because you've never tried it before. You will have to fail your way to success. So, what is required is not talent, though it helps. Neither is a genius IQ a prerequisite. All that is needed is the ability not to quit, to simply fail and keep coming back for more.

What it takes is a strong work ethic and the resilience to keep trying. You must learn to fail faster so that you can get up and try again faster. This will ultimately make you reach your goals faster. By knowing from the outset that you may fail multiple times attempting something helps remove the urgency that you simply must succeed the first time or else. This builds toughness and resilience, which later breeds confidence. This confidence reminds you not that you will necessarily succeed on the first try, but that you are okay if you don't.

By learning that you're not made of porcelain and that the world won't stop turning if you don't succeed initially, you can simply get up and try again. Only this time a little tougher and closer to your target- and again, until you find a better way to attempt the endeavor which eventually leads to your success. Success is equal parts organization, motivation, consternation, and determination regarding your destination.

Failing to Succeed

There are countless examples of "failures" who later became hugely successful because they kept going when others quit.

Abraham Lincoln was demoted from an officer to the lowest rank possible while serving in the military. He then failed multiple times in business. Even in politics, he was initially defeated and unimpressive, yet he went on to become the 16th President of the United States.

Theodor Seuss Geisel had his first book turned down by 27 publishers before someone took a chance on his "silly" book. Now Dr. Seuss' books have sold hundreds of millions worldwide.

Vincent Van Gogh is considered one of the most influential painters in modern history with a style that is immediately recognizable the world over. He created over 2000 pieces of art in his short 37 years of life, yet sold only one painting while he lived. His painting "Portrait of Dr. Gachet" sold for $82.5 million in 1990.

Muhammad Ali gave his first Olympic gold medal to the high school teacher who told him, "You ain't ever gonna be nothin."

If these people had stopped the first time they ever faced the Adversity of failure, the world would never have experienced the gifts that they had to offer.

"A journey of a thousand miles begins with a single step."

- Lao Tzu-

Using the simplistically single-minded mentality of Lao Tzu, I kept moving forward. I reminded myself that I wasn't trying to build a wall, I was simply trying to lay a single brick perfectly. By focusing on repeating this single task intently over and over, the wall would eventually appear.

On my path to recovery, I failed. A lot. I failed so many times I lost count. I stopped counting because the number of times I fell became depressing. If I'd have counted how many times I had fallen and failed to try to walk, it would have taken my attention away from the most important task at hand. My Primary Objective was learning to walk and use my hands again, not to count how many times I failed to attempt to do so. By not fixating on the number of times I failed and instead focused on how many times I was able to articulate my extremities correctly, I was positively reinforcing the thing I wanted to happen. If I kept track of how many times I failed, subconsciously I'd be doing myself a disservice. By focusing on the number of times I succeeded, I was exercising and reinforcing the habit of belief and mental follow-through.

Mental Follow-Through

An example of how mindset affects mental follow-through can be found with one of the most powerful land animals on earth, the elephant.

The classic story tells of a bystander seeing an adult elephant held in place by a small rope tied to its front leg. They ask the trainer why the elephant doesn't break free of this rope, as the rope clearly would not be able to hold the powerful animal. The trainer explains that as a baby, the elephant is tied by the same size rope, which at that time is too strong for the baby elephant to sever. As the small elephant tries with all its might to break free but cannot, this breaks the creature's will to escape. The same sized rope is then used to tie the elephant as it gets older, holding it in place without issue. As simple as escape sounds, an elephant never forgets that it tried as hard as it could to break free once and failed. It gave up trying to overcome this temporary Adversity, which caused it to give up trying for the rest of its life.

Humans are no different. We all know people who "were going to" to open a business, go to school or move to another city, but then never followed through with it. Why don't they? They realized that the action of trying to do these things was much more expensive than the price of talking about it. Perhaps someone told them that they couldn't do it or that it would simply be too hard even to attempt. The suggestion of potential Adversity can work on the human animal as well.

If someone told you that the door you were preparing to open was locked, when it was only a little stuck, you may not be able to open it. You couldn't open it because you believed what was suggested to you. You believed it to be locked. This is an example of a lack of mental follow through. This affects your level of commitment regarding your goal of opening the door. If you believe the door to be locked, then you give up and stop committing effort as soon as you feel the slightest amount of resistance, but if you were told the door wasn't locked, that it's only a little stuck before you ever touch the door handle, you'd know to pull through the temporary resistance and swing the door open. Thus, because of your mental commitment and belief, the door will open wide. This is a perfect illustration of how Adversity stops many from achieving their goals.

Everyone knows, though few want to admit, that to have anything worth having requires a certain amount of hard work and dedication. Generally speaking, the greater the goal, the greater the sacrifice required to achieve said goal.

Even though everyone is aware of this fact, there are still those who harbor certain misconceptions: "I know it's difficult, but I'm going to work TWICE as hard as all those other losers! (12 months later) Why am I not the CEO of my own multibillion dollar corporation yet!?"

"Yeah, yeah, yeah, Mr. Adversity Guy I get it. It's tough to be a successful (salesperson, product developer, entrepreneur, etc.) but I know something you don't. The secret is to work smarter, not harder! That's why I just bought (insert the name of hot, magical new product that teaches you to do it better, faster and easier than EVERYBODY else) and by using their patented four step process, I can't lose!"

Yes, everyone wants to work smarter, not harder. I see it every day. The creative that wants to be an artist or writer, but doesn't want to do so unless they "feel inspired," yet they aren't disciplined enough to "feel inspired" consistently enough to make a living at it.

The person who wants to open their own small business, but doesn't even so much as create a business plan to make legitimate strides in opening a business. So instead, they stay at the job they hate and bitch about it the entire time, yet continue to do nothing about it.

The person who does own a business and wants to make improvements in efficiency regarding everything from procedures to personnel, but never implements them consistently. Instead, they end up working in their business like an employee. Instead of owning the business, the business owns them. Of course, everyone wants to work smarter and not harder! Unfortunately for many, that seems to be code for "I don't actually want to have to work for it at all."

Smarter Not Harder

One of the first martial arts Bruce Lee studied seriously was Wing Chun Gung Fu under the legendary Grandmaster Ip Man. Wing Chun is a close range martial art that focuses on quick, explosive striking. The principles of Wing Chun set the foundation for what would later become Bruce Lee's martial expression, Jeet Kune Do.

During a seminar with world-renowned Wing Chun Sifu Francis Fong, he explained why his hands appeared to be so fast. For the record, Sifu Francis Fong's hands genuinely are incredibly fast! That's one of the big reasons they appear to be so fast. He went on to explain that his quickness was because of the efficiency of his movements, not simply his speed.

By having his hands constantly occupy centerline (the center of the opponent's body) he has less distance to travel to his intended target. Therefore, he can hit much faster due to sheer proximity. This economy of motion makes him more efficient, thus making his movements smarter. Or as Sifu Fong said so eloquently: "Don't work harder, work smarter. And when you learn to do it smarter, work hard at it."

Bartending Hotlanta

I first learned about how big of an impact even the smallest amount of efficiency could make while bartending in Atlanta. According to my Fitbit, it was easy to walk over 7 miles on a busy night behind the bar. Every wasted motion took precious time. I could see a direct correlation between my tips at the end of the night and how efficient I was at slinging drinks during my shift.

As an experiment, one night I had my bar back bring up two extra bottles of our most popular liquor. I placed the bottles strategically around my serving area so I was able to pour an ice-cold shot, regardless of where I stood. Even though it was only a small two steps to reach the singular bottle, having one within reach at all times had a large compounding effect. Instead of selling my usual three bottles a night, I was now pouring through 5 bottles without any greater perceived effort on my part. This efficiency allowed me to pour more shots faster, therefore creating more revenue and tips. Needless to say, I continued having the extra bottles brought up from that night forward.

With approximately 60 shots per bottle, this was an additional 120 shots served. With an average of $1 tip per ounce poured added an extra $120 per shift. With a conservative estimation of this happening twice a week that's an extra $960 a month. Over the course of a year, that

139

brought in an additional $11,000 without any increased effort. Smarter not harder indeed.

Like Francis Fong said, if I wasn't moving efficiently, I wasn't moving smartly, and making "dumb" movements was costing me money.

Protocols > Thoughts and Emotions

There is a way to work smarter and not harder, but it takes some time, effort, and forethought to do so. For some, at least in the beginning stages, this makes it feel like they are working harder and because of this, many will give up the practice.

Those who give up probably are working harder, but only because they are resistant to changing their habits. They are fighting against themselves, which is the opposite of smarter not harder.

In the military, there are Standard Operating Procedures (SOP's) put in place to minimize confusion in the heat of battle. When things fall apart as they inevitably will, you can fall back to the SOP's set-in-place so that when such a situation arises, you can act accordingly.

Old habits can be incredibly hard to break, which is why to work smarter and not harder, we must replace the old habits with protocols based on efficiency and consolidation instead of emotion and cognition. For example, something as simple as increasing the speed of the mouse on your computer to the highest tracking rate can make a huge difference over the long run. When you consider how often you are on your computer, those few seconds saved (once you've gotten used to the faster speed over a couple of days) over time will result in literally 1000's of hours saved over the course of your lifetime.

In poker, this type of thinking is imperative to becoming a winning player. By taking certain actions over and over to create a protocol or "standard play" causes you to act correctly and efficiently without a second thought. "Standard plays," such as raising every time you enter a pot, continuation betting on the flop, and stealing the blinds are all ways that you can play virtually on autopilot and still make money without having to battle your emotions or think twice about acting. Initially, these "standard plays" will seem forced and uncomfortable. These are all acquired behaviors that take some time to learn and implement continually to make it second nature. It is imperative to learn these poker lessons from the beginning; otherwise, you may lose your nerve when there's a lot of money to be won or lost on a single decision that should be second nature.

In negotiations, "highball" is a common tactic employed. This is done by asking for more than we are anticipating so that we have room to negotiate a price we want. One party will give a high price, then the other will counter with a "low ball" offer, and the dance of negotiation continues from there. On rare occasions, there will be times when you get what you were trying to highball for in the first place. Even if this only happens 10% of the time, this is a huge win and is well worth the effort of developing such strategies.

The same happens when we ask more of ourselves. This principle can be used when exercising. For example, if I don't know how many repetitions I can get with a certain amount of weight, I "highball" my estimation. If I set a goal of twenty repetitions, even if I only get seventeen, I still get more than if I'd set my sights lower at ten repetitions. Having high expectations creates greater output.

Like pouring more drinks at the bar, increasing the speed of your mouse, standard plays in poker and effective negotiation tactics, these protocols of efficiency pay huge dividends over time. The sooner you implement them, the faster you'll see returns on such investments.

Inhibition

Protocols can be used not only to create behaviors but also to inhibit other behaviors as well. For example, a deterrent is often a better motivator than a reward. With a reward, you must do something to 'win' it, but a deterrent discourages a particular behavior.

If you're trying to eat healthy, having junk food in the house should not even be an option. If you only give yourself choices that are healthy and adhere to your desired eating philosophy, you are much more likely to succeed. If you allow yourself an alternative, the drive-through burger joint for example, then you are now allowing yourself an opportunity to fail. The knowledge that you have food at home that is not only convenient but also healthy helps keep you on track.

These protocols let you minimize the thought process and choices to benefit you. This is especially helpful on days when you are mentally or physically fatigued and stressed out. Our diet and workouts are some of the first casualties to fall by the wayside when we are tired, frustrated, and stressed. When we get to the point that we are tired and hungry, it's easy to just want something to eat right now. Once we are at this point, eating healthy seems to be the least of our concerns. By not having junk food in your home, you are not deterred from eating it. If you are triggered by stress or fast food commercials, you now must actively go and seek it out. For some, their laziness will work in their favor, because they know they must go to all the effort required to acquire said junk food.

Just having bad food in the house in and of itself could act as a trigger for a temptation that could have otherwise been easily avoided. All it takes a moment of weakness to go off track, but if you have to get in the car, drive to your desired destination, and buy your junk food, then you have to make multiple decisions to cheat on your diet. (Deciding to get in the car, drive to the burger joint, buy the food, and consume it means you've made four separate decisions to go off your eating strategy.) By having to make the decision multiple times to eat unhealthy food gives you time and multiple opportunities to refocus on your goal of staying on your diet. This allows you to turn the car around metaphorically as well as literally. Having these protocols in place allow you to reinforce discipline without having to think about it. This surplus of discipline can then be used in other areas as it is needed.

The Fireplace or the Hunt

Midwestern winters aren't as bad as they are in the Northeast, but they can still get cold, wet, and miserable none the less. As an 11-year old boy going deer hunting for the first time, leaving the warmth of the fireplace before dawn was both new and exciting for me. Armed with our backpacks, rifles, and a thermos of coffee, we made our way through the snow and ice on a crisp winter morning.

If you spoke to my Uncle Ronnie, you'd never know he'd been in the service. He loved civilian life and was happily married to my great-aunt until the day he died. He never really spoke about his service, except to say that he was proud that he defended his country and the people he loved in it. A true quiet professional.

As he parked the truck, the freezing drizzle began to come down. We got out and started walking, me following my Uncle's footprints in the ½ foot of snow as best as my little legs could manage. The land we were hunting was nearly 100 acres, but my Uncle had done some recon and found the best place for us to set up. It was about a fifteen-minute walk to our location. As we walked, the freezing drizzle began to come down harder, eventually turning into sleet. By the time we got to our spot, I was a cold, wet, and miserable mess. We sat under cover of a large tree as we both took out our thermos from our backpacks. His filled with coffee, mine filled with hot tea. He took a sip of coffee as he looked at me, "You're shivering, are you cold?"

Soaking wet from head to toe, I shook my head in affirmation as my shaking hands cradled my honey sweetened hot tea to my freezing lips. He looked up at the overcast sky and said, "Well what do you want to do? We can go back if you're too cold."

Teeth chattering, I asked "Aren't you cold Uncle Ronnie? You look like the cold and rain doesn't bother you at all." He smiled and looked off into the distance for a moment.

**

1st Sergeant Ronald J. Pitts had served multiple tours in Vietnam with Special Forces Long Range Reconnaissance Patrol (LRRP). As a green beret and leader of an LRRP team, his leadership and knowledge of field craft was honed and well earned from dozens of missions. He had experienced many extremes in that life. From extreme weather and hunger to extreme fatigue and fear, this Adversity taught him how to become the eye of the storm.

**

Still smiling faintly, he replied, "I'm just as cold as you are, but I learned something a long time ago." He took another sip of coffee and continued. "Tell me, do you think the cold care about you?" he asked in a very matter of fact manner. Not mean or with even the slightest hint of condescension, just an innocent question. I thought for a second then said, "I guess it probably doesn't." "Correct. What you're thinking about is the cold, but what you should be thinking about isn't the cold, it's the hunt you should be focused on. Think more about what we are trying to accomplish and you will forget about the cold."

While this was easier said than done, what he said made perfect sense to me. "You have to understand, nature is neither for you nor against you, it simply is. It doesn't care about you one way or the other. There are no rewards, there are no punishments, there are simply consequences. So, which do you want more, the fireplace or the hunt?" Still shivering and cold, I was torn. I wanted to be strong like my Uncle, but the warm fireplace sounded very inviting at the moment. "What do you want to do Uncle Ronnie?" "The decision is yours," he said, "but I'll tell you this much—the fireplace will always be there. It's safe and warm, a sure thing; but, there's no opportunity to bring home meat if we don't go out and hunt." He finished his cup of joe then added, "We're already cold and wet, so we've already suffered the hardship of the hunt. We might as well try to get something for our efforts. Sound good to you?"

This change in perspective was all the encouragement I needed. I focused on the possibilities to be gained from the hunt instead of our current miserable, but temporary, conditions. We stayed out in the freezing drizzle for a few more hours, and then we eventually called it a day. Neither of us shouldered our weapon or fired a shot. We didn't even see a deer, but from the hunt, I still brought home a great prize. The prize was the tremendous lesson I learned from this exercise in hardship. That shift in mindset changed everything for me. Understanding this lesson in what I now recognize to be modern Stoicism helped shape me into the person I am today. Later in my life, I'd hear echoes of this ethos from SSG Basil Reid as well. In the end, it all comes down to one thing: Discipline.

Discipline

"Don't count on motivation, count of discipline."

-Jocko Willink-

Discipline is the ultimate protocol. Motivation will fade, let discipline take its place. By keeping the overarching principle of discipline at the forefront of your decision making, vicariously you can make the best choices without even having to think about it. This helps you concentrate on the things of actual importance instead of chasing your tail on less pressing tasks.

By choosing to avoid the temptation of doing that which is "easy" (and subsequently less important) you will be focused on the things that are worth doing by default. Don't make success harder than it needs to be. If your default choice always comes back to choosing discipline, you will always begin in the right place. This mentality makes discipline the standard.

Conditions may change, but standards remain. Continually making the disciplined choice creates momentum that helps propel you forward, building speed without any additional effort. This momentum is like free energy that you can do with as you wish. You can continue to build more momentum by adding it to your previous efforts, or the momentum can help push you through if you happen to miss a step or slow down momentarily in your endeavors. Discipline is simply motivation put into action over and over again.

Comparison may indeed be the thief of joy, but it is the creator of excellence. I understand that we are all unique individuals. I also agree that you are your only competition. With that said, you should be pushing yourself harder than any outside competitor can or ever will. You know the areas where you are slacking, the areas where you need improvement. Stop waiting for somebody else to point them out to you, stop waiting for permission to begin. Identify the areas needing improvement, even if it is something small, and get to work. You will find even the smallest improvement can create momentum and self-confidence.

Discipline is delaying short-term pleasure for a greater reward later. That's why it's paramount to start goal setting from a place of enthusiasm because it allows you to dream unfettered by fatigue or stress. This mindset is imperative to let dreams and goals grow as lofty as possible. This is what makes the objective desirable in the first place. Discipline like any skill is perishable. It must be exercised regularly and honed continually in order to improve. Learn to master your will, then leverage it to override the body and mind's objections to the inevitable hard work needed to progress ever forward. Discipline is logical. It relies more on our consistency than some passing emotion. Motivation is primarily emotional, which is why it varies from moment to moment. Discipline is well thought out, constant and unrelenting. Discipline leads to organization. The secret to success is preparation born from discipline. Organization from discipline forces one to do what needs to be done when it needs to be done, whether we feel like it or not. Your goals don't give a damn about how you feel. Everybody wants to become a "success," but few want to put in the amount of work necessary to become one. It all boils down to a single question: Do you want to accomplish your goals, or do you want to do what is comfortable at this moment?

The things you want to achieve and acquire will require a tremendous amount of consistent, disciplined effort. This will be difficult; it's supposed to be that way. If it were easy, you wouldn't respect it. We must be willing to give up something that we value greatly to achieve that which is of even greater value. You are investing your time, effort, and mental energy into something that you know will be even greater, and it can be yours for a price, but the price of greatness is discipline.

Discipline makes you seize the present to create the future.

Discipline is nothing more than the ability to give yourself a command and then seeing it through to fruition. It's not about what you want to do. It's not about what you'd rather do, it's about what needs to be done NOW and making it happen. You don't have to WANT to do the work, but it still must be done in to achieve the great things you truly want and desire.

Discipline is focused. It's easy to rush from one task to another because you are momentarily enthused, but discipline is what is left when you no longer feel excited to do what you set out to do from your initial state of motivation. I am not magical. I am not special. I am not unique.

What I am is disciplined—and through discipline, my results appear magical, special, and unique- especially to the undisciplined.

Discipline is what separates the mediocre from the great.

I acknowledge that there are certain times randomness can come into play, but for the most part, discipline is what gets us where we want to go. Just because a person happens to win the lottery is the exception that proves the rule. Yes, luck smiled on the person who won, but for the other 99.99%, it's back to work Monday morning. I for one would rather apply my efforts towards something I have control over than towards something as random as luck. I can control my work ethic, and I've noticed that the harder I work, the more opportunities present themselves. I don't call that luck; I call it discipline put into action.

Discipline is uncommon.

Discipline is in short supply. This fact makes it all the more valuable a commodity. Many of the products sold today are bought by people in hopes that it will be a substitute for their lack of discipline. Whether it be a weight loss supplement that doesn't require you to exercise change your diet, a piece of workout equipment that promises to make you look like a fitness model in a week, or a program that teaches you how to flip houses making six digits in six months- these things are not bought by people, they are purchased by the laziness of people. The promise of incredible rewards with almost no effort separates a fool from their money quickly and repeatedly.

The fact that so many are undisciplined, unorganized, and unaware gives those that exercise discipline a HUGE ADVANTAGE in any enterprise. Through discipline, all things are possible, without discipline nothing worth doing gets accomplished.

Make Discipline a habit. It is your mental tenacity that dictates your capacity. Turn discipline into a habit, and it will eventually present itself in all facets of your life. Weakness in one area is often an indication of lack of discipline in other.

Missing work deadlines, not studying for a class, and procrastination, in general, all come back to a lack of consistent discipline. So, by telling yourself that slipping "just this once" on your diet, personal development planning, or workout schedule isn't a big deal, you couldn't be more wrong.

It's a huge deal, and it works both ways. There will be plenty of situations in life that will slow your progress and potentially throw you off-track. Don't let your lack of discipline be one of those things.

You'll come to find that when you're disciplined in the other aspects of your life, you don't feel tempted to cheat on your diet, your work productivity schedule, or significant other for that matter. Discipline then no longer becomes a choice, it's just something you do subconsciously. Discipline then becomes a habit, and that habit becomes the new standard.

Practice Does Not Make Perfect

One night, a student came to the academy early to work on the heavy bag before Jeet Kune Do class. Before he began, he looked at me and smiled saying "practice makes perfect Sifu." I watched the student punch for a few moments, then continued preparing for class.

That evening, the first combination I taught was very simple; the jab, cross. The "1,2" is a fundamental punching combination that is taught from day one. I showed the combo once, asked if there were any questions, and gave everyone a two-minute round to work it. You can tell how serious a student is by how they perform the most rudimentary techniques. There were some in class who had done this simple combination for years, yet they still attacked it with precision and intensity. Others may overlook the necessity of doing such "basic techniques," and therefore, may not take these fundamentals seriously. The student's mentality in this regard becomes apparent within moments of them performing the combination.

After the class had performed the combination for their allotted time, I asked: "Practice makes what?" "Perfect!" was the universal response I was greeted by. I smiled at the class and said no. I looked at the puzzled, sweaty faces for a moment before I continued. "Practice does not make perfect; it makes permanent."

Some of the students seemed to comprehend, but others still looked understandably confused. "Practice doesn't make perfect; it makes permanent. Only perfect practice creates perfection in application."

I could do a technique for ten years, but if I've done it incorrectly for that amount of time, not only is it biomechanically incorrect, it's now been hardwired into my mind and body that way. In the above punching example, if I drop one of my hands when I throw the jab-cross and allow that to become a habit, that's how I will attempt to execute the punches in combat. By practicing the technique incorrectly because I'm not fulling engaged physically and mentally, I'm now making the technique permanent. In this case, permanently flawed, and the student may not even be aware of it. This small flaw may not seem like a big deal, but it is not only inefficient, it's potentially dangerous.

There is no martial art technique that is full proof. If I execute a strike, do a takedown, apply a submission, or utilize a weapon there is always an area left vulnerable. One of the best times to counter attack someone is while they are in the process of the attack itself. When they are in attack mode, very few are thinking of simultaneously defending. While sheer aggression may work against an untrained individual, dropping your non-punching hand while you attack a trained opponent is a great way to get knocked out.

The reality is, there are no advanced techniques in the martial arts, there are only fundamental techniques that can be done well under the Adversity of conflict. The more complicated the technique or combination of techniques, the more likely it is to fail you under the pressure of combat. This is Occam's Razor put into action.

What Do You Think?

"Excellence is an art won by training and habituation. We do not act rightly because we have virtue or excellence, but we rather have those because we have acted rightly. We are what we repeatedly do. Excellence, then, is not an act but a habit."

-Aristotle-

In the book "The Power of Habit" by Charles Duhigg, he cites a paper published by a Duke University researcher in 2006 that found more than 40 percent of the actions people performed each day were habits. This means that nearly half of our behaviors are done without making a conscientious decision. While I understand that not every action we do requires our utmost concentration (brushing our teeth, getting dressed, eating, etc.) this insight into human behavior is still very telling. This applies to our mental habits as well.

Mental Practice to Make Permanent

It's the thoughts we repeatedly think that have the greatest effect on our lives. Thinking positively will take practice, which explains why it's important to be mindful of your thoughts from moment to moment. We have thousands of thoughts in the background of our mind, both positive and negative, every day. These thoughts create multiple repetitions, and these repetitions are what makeup practice, whether we are aware of it or not.

We often think of practice as a purely physical act, but creating and repeating thought patterns are practiced acts as well. Practice doesn't make perfect; it makes permanent. Make sure the thought patterns you're hardwiring into your mind are positive and will help you over the long run. There are enough negative things to contend with in life, don't let your thoughts be one of them.

Allow your thoughts to act as a positive backdrop for everything you do. If you are constantly in a state of chaos, guess what you're repeating and practicing mentally hundreds of times a day? You guessed it; you're reinforcing chaos and all the negativity attached to it. This can become a self-fulfilling prophecy, and it will eventually become a repeating cycle. Instead, you think of having gratitude, being resilience, or feeling love, those will be the thoughts repeating over and over in your subconscious mind, and it will program you to see and expect these positive things to come to pass.

When I talk about thinking positively, I need to be more specific. I don't mean that you are in an artificial, happy-go-lucky mindset all the time. This type of fake positivity is the intellectual equivalent of hiding your head in the sand. It does little to further your growth and help you achieve your goals. Instead of viewing a mindset as "positive" or "negative," choose to see it from a less judgmental viewpoint.

When viewing your thoughts, simply see if they are constructive. Ask yourself: "Are these thoughts and actions constructive to my goals? Are they bringing me closer to my primary objectives?" If they are not constructive, then change them without wasting emotion and energy deeming them "good or evil." It does little good to view thoughts as "nonconstructive" or even a "destructive" category, this would be a form of judging that will reinforcement a negative mindset.

When I was learning to walk again, I didn't want to reinforce the times I fell by "judging" myself and my actions as either a success or failure. Instead, I use this mindset as a means of keeping me focused and on task. If we judge our thoughts as being nonproductive, there is often a cascade of additional nonconstructive thoughts that flow from this single form of negativity. For example, if you are aggravated for not progressing as quickly as you wanted to on a particular project, it could cause you to second guess yourself. This can cause an avalanche of other negative emotions that ultimately will not be beneficial to you in the long run.

3 of 6

Dr. Marshall Goldsmith is in a class all his own. Known as the #1 Leadership and CEO coach in the world, this New York Times bestselling author has created massive positive change in multiple Fortune 500 companies. He charges $250,000 for this service and has a money back guarantee, that tells you how good he is at his job! In Dr. Goldsmith's remarkable book "Triggers" he has a list of questions that should be asked every day as a form of self-monitoring.

Here are Dr. Goldsmith's six questions:

Did I do my best to set clear goals?

Did I do my best to make progress towards goal achievement?

Did I do my best to build positive relationships?

Did I do my best to find meaning?

Did I do my best to be happy?

Did I do my best to be fully engaged?

By having these questions fresh in mind, they help keep you purpose driven with your time. Remember, these are questions that are meant to keep us focused on effort, not necessarily on the result of said effort.

While these questions are a great way to stay mentally focused, for some, they can be overwhelming. The questions cover a huge amount of ground that requires a tremendous amount of mental energy. While these questions are incredibly thorough, they can seem daunting, especially when the answer to some of these questions seem to be a consistent and resounding "no."

If being aware of all these questions seems like too much initially, you can modify them to be more user-friendly. Think of these modifications as training wheels to get you started or maybe you'll like the condensed version more than the original six questions. You may even create your own modified version; the key is to find what works best for you and then utilize it.

First, instead of thinking of these as simple yes or no questions, think of them as statements that can be used to encourage the focus of your thoughts.

For example, instead of asking "Did I do my best to set clear goals today?" turn the question into a statement, such as, "set clear goals today" or "I will set clear goals today." This takes away any negative connotations associated with answering "no" to your question. Remember, if we are honest, the answer will be "no" most of the time. But that's why the questions are in place; there's a difference between achieving and trying. We won't always achieve the desired "yes" but we can always try to improve, and that's the real goal.

Another way to start implementing this protocol is to reduce the number of statements used. For example, find the three of the six questions that will cover the most ground and perhaps even answer the rest of the questions.

Look at the following statements:

Set clear goals for today.

Focus on working towards achieving those goals.

Stay fully engaged.

Notice again that these are the original questions put into a statement form. These thoughts become your mantra of focus throughout the day. By having only three things to concentrate on, it allows greater focus to make them happen.

But what about the other three questions? Are they less important? No, they are very important. The other three questions or statements will be addressed, but indirectly.

The three questions left out were:

Did I do my best to build positive relationships?

Did I do my best to find meaning?

Did I do my best to be happy?

How do we answer these important questions indirectly?

The answer to these last three questions is found in how we address the first three statements. By staying focused on achieving the first three statements, the last three questions take care of themselves incidentally.

When we set clear goals, focus on achieving those goals, and stay fully engaged these things lead to building positive relationships, finding meaning, and being happy.

If three questions seem like too much to handle, narrow it down to the two that need immediate improvement and mean the most to you. Even if you can only focus on one, that is still progress. For example, if simply focusing on staying fully engaged helps you, then start there. After you've become conditioned to use this one principle, slowly add the others as you are able. Utilize the 80/20 principle to make Dr. Goldsmith's wisdom work for you.

Power of Mindset

As I touched on in previous chapters, many preach that the only thing needed to be successful in life, business, and any other endeavor is a positive mindset. The reality is that having a strong, positive mindset is not only an absolute necessity, it's the bare minimum for success.

That's like saying the only thing you need to build a great house is a foundation. While a solid foundation is imperative, it is only the beginning. Without walls or a roof, it is nothing more than underutilized potential. A positive mindset is merely a prerequisite to achieving your goals. Without it, your success will be short-lived at best. Think of your mindset as the foundation of your future success in anything.

Mindset and Discipline > Motivation

When I was told I'd never walk again, the quote that opened this chapter immediately sprang to mind. It was with Hannibal's mindset of "finding a way or making one" that made me commit completely and totally to recovering. Fear of never walking again was a huge driving force, but I also saw my injury as the ultimate challenge. Again, this is what Adversity does for us when we see it as such, as a means to motivate us to endeavor further than we ever conceived possible.

I saw my Adversity as a gift, I learned to embrace it. I saw it as the catalyst needed to create the change I so desperately sought after.

You must learn to love the challenge because it's the price that must be paid repeatedly to become the best you can be at anything. Discomfort is the requirement for any growth worth having.

In this life, there is always something we must grapple with, that we must resist. Be it the temptation to be lazy and not push ourselves or a more daunting form of Adversity, there is an omnipresent résistance that we must overcome. Either you fight now to gain what you want, or fight later to maintain what you currently possess.

"You have power over your mind - not outside events.
Realize this, and you will find strength."

-Marcus Aurelius-

When I worked at a job that I hated, the time would drag by, and I'd feel lethargic, but as soon as I clocked out, I'd feel immediately relieved and revitalized. This shows that I wasn't physically tired, but being at a job that I didn't really care about actually caused mental and physical fatigue. For instance, seriously consider your emotional response to each of the following three scenarios:

1. After work, you're going out with some co-workers to celebrate your bonuses from your newest business deal!

2. After work, you have to work on your taxes for the next three hours to get them filed without penalty.

3. Just kidding nothing's changed, you can do whatever you already had planned to do tonight.

Each scenario causes an almost visceral response when taken seriously. The first one probably creates excitement.

The second scenario, on the other hand, probably causes dread and the makings of a migraine. Finally, the third likely causes relief just by comparison to the mentally taxing burden of doing your taxes.

Isn't it interesting how good a "boring night at home" sounds in contrast to something we loathe? Did you notice how your mentality created a change in your feelings, emotions, and energy levels regarding each of the scenarios? How exactly did this happen? Nothing physically happened to you, right? What caused these reactions? Who gave you this incredible power that lets you experience these emotions by thinking of them? You guessed it, YOU DID. More to the point, your thoughts made this happen. The power of your belief made these emotions real, and ultimately, who controls your thoughts, and therefore, emotions? That's right, YOU DO. This is an amazing ability; it sounds almost superhuman does it not?

If you possess the power to make a situation worse mentally, and you do, then you have the same power to make it better. Ultimately, you are the one in control of your thoughts and emotions. Before my injury, I thought that I was strong in some capacities, but now that I'd started to overcome my injuries to an extent, I learned that I am far stronger than I ever imagined. In the end, we are only as strong as the Adversity that we overcome.

Is it Really?

It is so easy to complain about anything and everything from the weather, to your job, to your relationships. Those who complain the most do so because they don't appreciate the things that they have. So, the next time you catch yourself in this cycle of complaining about everything, stop for a moment and ask yourself an honest question: Is the what you're complaining about really that bad? Is it really?

Is it the most difficult thing you've ever faced in your life? Chances are it's probably not. As a matter fact 99.99% of the time, it will not be the most difficult thing you've ever had to do in your life.

Adversity is the catalyst that forces us to adapt and improve, generally in a manner that we would not seek out voluntarily if left to our own devices. After we've overcome our Adversity, we are not only stronger, we are wiser than before. This unearths in us a resilience that would otherwise lie dormant had we not been pressed to find it. I now use this question as a gauge.

When I'm about to embark on a seemingly difficult task, I stop and think of the hardest thing I've ever experienced in my life. I then compare that Adversity to the task at hand. And as if by magic, the task withers in comparison.

Fearless to Fear-less

My Adversity introduced me to my actual strength. This newfound knowledge gave me a sense of confidence to be more fearless than I'd ever thought possible. I'm not crazy; I'm just no longer afraid. Honestly, I now feel fearless. Not because I am without fear per se, on the contrary, I have plenty- but there are many kinds of fear. The fear that possesses me now is the fear of not achieving what I want to in the time that remains. Again, it's not that I am without fear, but the animosity of not accomplishing all the things I long for in this life is far greater any potential future trepidation.

Fear is only as real as we believe it to be, as we allow it to be. With this truth in mind, I use fear as my compass. Before I embark on any endeavor worthy of my time— meaning a lofty goal or challenge, I ask myself a question to put things in perspective: What's the worst that can happen? Is what I'm about to attempt going to kill or cripple me? Probably not.

This makes me feel like I have nothing to lose because I don't. I've already felt the pain of losing EVERYTHING I ever cared about once; I'll NEVER go back to that place again, mentally or physically. After all that I've been through and overcome, why would I settle for anything less than my greatest possible efforts now?

I've only just begun to catch a glimpse of my actual potential, I WILL NOT sit back idly and let this second opportunity pass me by. You must appreciate that fortune favors those who dare to reach for their goals, and our reach should always exceed our grasp. Many have overcome much more than you face now, and they did so with far less than you currently possess. Whatever your excuse is, someone else has overcome it. Whatever your fear may be, someone has gained strength from conquering it.

Of course, the biggest challenge of having this perspective is trying to maintain it at the moment. It's very easy to be philosophical about someone else's pain. Yet, when that same pain or something greater befalls us, it's much more difficult to be rational. Bear this in mind now so that you might implement it during times of your own misfortune.

The odds are in your favor because while everyone wants to achieve great things, or at least claims to, very few will make the sacrifices needed to achieve success. This does not mean it will be easy. In fact, it will be the hardest thing you've ever done in your life. It will cause you to question yourself, your will, and your motivation constantly. It will require you to fight with everything you possess to reach your destination.

There is but one level of commitment—total. You've got what it takes to succeed, but it will take absolutely everything you've got.

161

Adversity, like everything in life, is relative. It is your mindset that separates actual Adversity from mere aggravation, gut-wrenching pain from subtle discomfort, love that you would kill or die for from simple infatuation. Commit completely, believe irrefutably, achieve definitively.

Chapter IX

First Class

*"Everything we hear is an opinion, not a fact. Everything
we see is perspective, not the truth."*

-Marcus Aurelius-

May 2, 2011, was the day that I reported for duty at Ft.
Drum, New York, home of 10th Mountain Light Infantry
Division. I specify the date because it was a day that was
important not only to me but would prove to be a day of
significance to the nation.

My flight left early that Monday morning, and of course, I
had to be there an hour and a half early to be sure I'd catch
my flight. Missing your flight and not making it to your duty
station the first day would be a terrible first impression. I
got to the airport at 04:45, and it was a ghost town. That's
fine, I'd much rather be early than late. I had a connecting
flight to Chicago, then on to New York City to get my flight
to Upstate New York.

Traveling in my ACU's (Army Combat Uniform) made me
stand out, but I was told to wear them when I reported for

duty. The flight wasn't even half full when I boarded, and a stewardess was gracious enough to offer me a seat in first class. I politely declined, but one of the pilots just happened to be standing there and he was very insistent that I take the seat. As soon as we were airborne, I promptly fell asleep. I was out for what seemed only a moment when I heard the captain over the intercom telling us to prepare for landing.

As I walked into Chicago's O'Hare Airport with my duffle over my shoulder and sleep still in my eyes, I heard people start cheering and applauding. I thought nothing of it and kept moving forward. As I walked further, the cheering grew as did the applause. I now saw people pointing in my general direction. I turned to look behind me to see what all the commotion was about. Is there a celebrity in the airport? The people behind me began to cheer and point as well. Who are they cheering for?

Everyone around was clapping and pointing...at me!

Chants of "USA, USA!" echoed all around me. As I got past the dividers, overjoyed people rushed up to shake my hand like I was some sort of Rockstar. Complete strangers from all walks of life were hugging me, cheering, and patting me on the back.

Is this how they treat everyone in uniform? As I was being hugged by another group of joyous strangers, I could finally see what was causing this reaction.

My heart sank.

On every TV screen was the same breaking news story. My boss, the commander in chief of the United States Armed Forces, President Obama, was telling the world that we'd finally killed Osama Bin Laden.

(Subsequently, the following year President Obama came to Ft. Drum to announce to the United States that he was "bringing the troops home." He was making good on one of his original election promises, which just so happened to occur while he was running for his second term. This meant that 10th Mountain was not going to be deployed anytime soon. He announced this not long after I was injured. Call it schadenfreude if you will, but I felt a sense of selfish satisfaction knowing that the other men I'd trained so hard with wouldn't get to go to battle without me.)

After seeing the news, everything now made sense. I felt horrible. Everyone around me was congratulating me like I was the soldier who got Bin Laden, but I hadn't done anything. In fact, I wasn't even at my duty station yet! I hadn't deployed or earned any of this recognition.

More and more people kept coming up as I walked through the airport asking for pictures, giving me bottles of water and food like I was a hero. I was beside myself, completely overwhelmed. The people who deserved this were the people deployed, those who had done their job. The SEAL's were the ones who got Bin Laden; I wasn't even in the same branch of service!

As before, when I boarded the plane, they offered to put me in first class. Again, I respectfully declined. This time the flight was full, so I thought I was safe from the further embarrassment of being paraded up to first class, but a gentleman who was in first class saw me and insisted that I take his seat. He made it very clear that he wasn't taking no for an answer. Finally, I sheepishly accepted just to stop all the commotion.

Unlike the last flight, as soon as we were airborne, I couldn't sleep a wink. I was stricken with guilt. I felt like an imposter.

These people all saw me as a soldier who was either going off to war or just returning from battle, but I had done neither; I had done nothing to deserve their respect and admiration.

The man who had insisted on giving me his seat suddenly appeared out of nowhere with a beer in each hand, cheerfully handing one to me. Honestly, I don't even drink, but I knew to decline his offer would be a seen as disrespectful. I reached out for the beer. As his smile grew, so did my feeling of unworthiness. As he gave me the beer, he said, "Thank you SO MUCH for your service!" I couldn't take it anymore; the guilt was killing me. I was going to have to say something, but before I could say anything, he kept talking. "My nephew is currently deployed. So, giving you my seat and buying you a beer is the least I can do!"

That's when it hit me.

All this attention, accolades and well wishes, they weren't about me at all. These people were acting like this because of what I represented to them. When they saw the news and then immediately saw me walking by, they weren't cheering for me; they were cheering for all the other soldiers who were fighting. While they were hugging me physically, they were embracing what the uniform embodied. To them, I represented a father, son, brother, uncle, nephew or other family members who were currently, or who had previously, served in the military. From their perspective, I represented this victory. None of this was about me in the least; it was about what I stood for.

This knowledge took a huge weight off my shoulders. I was now able to thank the gentleman in first class with a smile on my face. I asked him more about his nephew, and we had a nice conversation before he headed back to his seat, my assigned seat. I was finally given a few moments to try to process the gravity of this historic day.

It made me think of soldiers in the past. I remembered seeing pictures of huge parades with people filling the streets, waving the American flag, and welcoming home the troops from World War I and II. The famous picture of the sailor kissing the nurse in Time Square came to mind. However, I also knew how the soldiers who returned from Vietnam were treated and was nothing like the reception I was receiving.

When my Great Uncle returned from Vietnam, there were huge anti-war demonstrations in the streets. People called him "baby killer." Some even tried to punch and spit on him. But he soldiered Stoically forward. He understood, as I now did, that they were acting from their own perspective, and their perspective did not make it the truth. I realized that this outpouring of love and admiration could easily go the other direction, and this knowledge gave me perspective as well.

Another Perspective

"Don't be in a hurry to condemn...because he doesn't do what you do or think as you think...There was a time when you didn't know what you know today."

-Malcolm X-

Adversity forces us to see things from a different perspective, a perspective that we'd never seek out voluntarily, and it's almost impossible to genuinely see that perspective any other way.

To grow, we must be willing to be uncomfortable. We must put ourselves in uncomfortable situations and have uncomfortable conversations to see beyond our current point of view. By discussing and seeing things from a different perspective, we are offered the chance of "controlled discomfort" without having to remain in that position permanently. This lets us collect knowledge otherwise unknown to us. This is why lively discussion and civil debate about a subject with friends and family can broaden one's horizons, but it must be handled correctly.

When people disagree about a subject, especially one that they hold dear, you must take into consideration how this person potentially sees your act of disagreement. That's why you never discuss religion or politics at a bar.

To understand where a person is coming from, you must first look at the other person's values and life experiences. Appreciate that their thoughts are, in some ways, very different than your own. This is because their past experiences are, in many ways, very different than yours.

Even if you do not agree with their reality or lifestyle, it is still their reality irrespective of your opinion. So, if you want them to respect your point of view, you must first act in kind. Listening intently is one of the greatest forms of respect you can give somebody.

Never enter such a discussion with a "holier than thou" attitude, as if you are the only one in the conversation to have an enlightened mentality. This closed off mindset automatically makes an opposing view somehow intellectually beneath you. There's nothing more infuriating than someone belittling your opinion because they think or assume they are smarter.

Having this predetermined mentality only makes those with a contrary view reciprocate the same prejudices. They feel like their point of view is misunderstood, because their specific story of what they went through goes unheard. Therefore, many get upset when someone disagrees with their opinion, because to them, it's more than just their opinion that you disagree with; they feel another is judging them by what they believe in, by their lifestyle. To them, it may seem as if you disapprove of how they were raised and what they were taught. Therefore, it seems as if you disagree with their parents and environment that taught such behavior. It's as if you disagree with everything about them. This is because emotions are in play, and emotions need to be taken out of the equation to understand another's point of view completely.

While in such situations, never be afraid to ask someone to clarify things for you to better understand their viewpoint. Ask them to clarify and ask "why." There's no need to feel intellectually insecure if your intent is a genuine understanding of their perspective.

This sort of candor helps us appreciate and understand another's point of view, even if we don't agree with it. This other point of view helps us learn about the motivations of others. These insights can teach us something new about the subject we are discussing. Seeing from an opposing viewpoint helps us see how they view our perspective. It also helps us see where our point of view or opinion is potentially lacking and in need of improvement.

For far too long, I looked at the world as having two sides. I thought you couldn't like both Coke and Pepsi. If you have a Conservative viewpoint about one subject, you can't have a Liberal one for another. If you are X, then you can't like Y and so on.

While brand loyalty is admirable, it has its shortcomings. Rarely have I seen one side of any argument be completely right without exception.

Generally, both sides will have an element of truth, and to throw the baby out with the bathwater is incredibly short-sighted.

Instead, why not look at the current needs of the situation and decide the best plan of action? Going into a situation with no preconceived notions to bias our outlook allows one to make the best decision without dogma, emotion, or ideology interfering. Stop drinking to Kool-Aide people.

This learning lets us walk around a subject and look at it from a different point of view, from another's point of view, an opposing view. This helps us better understand another's perspective.

With this newly learned information, we now have an additional way to potentially solve the problem at hand. We now have more than one way to skin the preverbal cat. Instead of having only two options, we now know a third potential, which is a combination of the best elements of the previous two. This, in turn, leads to a potential 4th possibility that may be a combination of the 2nd and 3rd, a 5th possibility is a combo of the 4th and 3rd and so on.

I learned a tremendous amount about perspectives from doing my TEDx talk at the TEDxCoMo event "Citizen." It's refreshing to see things in a different light. The stories and experiences of others help shed new light on subjects that I thought I already knew very well.

Even if you are unable to make it to a big event like TED or TEDx, that's still no excuse in today's age of information and technology. You have thousands of ideas, points of view and TED talks at your fingertips on the web if you so desire.

I have found that there's not a single person whose perspective I can agree with 100% of the time, every time, on anything as time wears on. This includes my own perspectives as they evolve.

The truth is unchanging, but our understanding of it is ever evolving, because we are ever evolving.

Guro

"I'm constantly learning all the time. Once you stop being a student, you stop growing."

-Guro Dan Inosanto, Bruce Lee's Protégé, Jeet Kune Do and Kali Master, 4x Black Belt Magazine Hall of Fame inductee-

Dan Inosanto grew up in Stockton California as a member of the Filipino "Bridge Generation." Inosanto started to learn boxing at the age of five, and the Martial Arts have been an integral part of his life ever since. Earning his Black Belt in American Kempo Karate from Ed Parker, Inosanto was introduced to Bruce Lee in August of 1964. He would later assist Bruce during the subsequent demonstrations that followed.

Guro Inosanto went on to become the Jeet Kune Do instructor at the Chinatown school opened by Lee in 1967. Inosanto was also immortalized on screen with Bruce Lee in the legendary nunchaku fight scene in "The Game of Death."

(Guro Inosanto is 82 years old at the time of this writing and continues to travel all over the world teaching seminars in addition to teaching at his academy in Marina Del Ray, California.)

During an instructor's camp at the Inosanto Academy, Guro taught a lesson about the necessity of perspective. Inosanto told us, "There are around 67 recognized judo throws, but most competitors will only use 3-5. These are the throws that they've perfected and that work the best for them." However, the competitors are still very aware of the other 60+ throws. They maintain this perspective for a couple of reasons.

One reason is that if the first throw they attempt fails, they will need a contingency throw, a Plan B. The second, and possibly more important reason is so they won't be victimized by the other throws. To be ignorant of this knowledge would leave a huge blind spot.

Machiavellian?

The pejorative "Machiavellian" is synonymous with cunning, scheming, and treachery; but upon closer examination, it seems Machiavelli may have gotten a bad rap.

Machiavelli's political opus "The Prince" wasn't released to the public until 1513, which was five years after his death. Niccolò Machiavelli wasn't all bad. In fact, he wrote, "The Prince" as more of a cautionary tale than anything.

In it, he tells how treacherous rulers had used their lack of morals and desire to "be feared" more than their need "to be loved" to manipulate and stay in power. However, this did not mean that he felt or acted in such manner.

In his book "Thick Black Theory," published in 1911, Li Zongwu spoke of similar methods used by Chinese politicians of his day. He wrote of the ruler Cao Cao who claimed: "I would rather betray someone than be betrayed." After being published, the book was quickly banned. In 1994, Chin-Ning Chu wrote the bestselling book, "Thick Face, Black Heart" based on Zongwu's "Thick Black Theory."

There are things I would never even think of doing to another person. Some strategies and manipulation so cutthroat, that they'd never even cross my mind. However, to some, it is this very knowledge that gives them the edge over those who think morally. So, while thinking diabolical thoughts isn't in my nature, I must learn to take them into consideration. Not because I may think or act in such a manner, but because others may use these brutal tactics against me.

This harkens back to the Judo competitors. They practice many different throws to be aware of them, even if they only use a handful themselves. This gives them a glimpse into a potential opponent's playbook, which in turn, helps them prepare a defense. Similarly, I don't necessarily want to use the unscrupulous methods of Machiavelli and Zongwu; but I need to know and understand them so that I don't fall prey to them.

If you want to learn something new, read an old book. Generally, the older, the better. Many of the books that have anything worth teaching have already been bastardized and cut up into pieces that are hardly recognizable now. Often, these bits of information and wisdom lose their significance. A tremendous amount of their meaning is watered down because they are either taken out of context to an extent or the strength of the lesson is lessened because the rest of the book helps create a more compelling overall argument; and because of this, the full gravity of the information is lost on the reader. Therefore, it is imperative to research your own experiences. Compare what you've learned to the writings of these classic works. See what writings ring true to you. This will give you a point of view that others aren't as easily and readily exposed to. This will afford you your own unique perspective, and this is how the thoughts that revolutionize the world often come about.

Published in 1974, "Winning Through Intimidation" By Robert J. Ringer offers some keen insights as well. While the book is technically written about real estate, the pragmatic lessons about business harken back to shades of Machiavelli and "Thick Black Theory".

One of the common threads in the book is having the ability to simply let go and walk away when you realize the situation no longer serves you. He'd gained this perspective from years of failed business deals and thousands of negotiations.

Ringer states: "There is no one deal, person, or situation that will completely make or break your life."

Though this lesson may be difficult to stomach, this perspective is incredibly liberating. Having this knowledge relieves us from fearing every possible interaction's ultimate success or failure. Having the ability to simply say to ourselves, "Next!" when what we're working on is a lost cause, allows us to act unencumbered. It lets you act naturally and comfortably within any situation, which is always the most genuine version of yourself. It also saves us time and energy in the future.

It reminds us not to lose sleep over missed opportunities of the past but encourages us to make the most of every possible opportunity we're given now this moment. Absolute certainty is rarely gained in the things that we desire most. All we can do is prepare as best we can with the knowledge and skills that we possess currently, the rest is out of our control.

Look at your life, look at the situation that you are currently in. And ask yourself, "What is this an opportunity for? What am I supposed to be learning in this situation, what is the lesson here?"

Understand that there is an opportunity in everything we do and everything that we experience, be it positive or negative. The universe has a way of trying to teach a lesson, and if the lesson isn't mastered, it will be something you encounter over and over again. And while the exact situation may be a little different each time, the lesson is still present. So, if I don't learn how to read for example, and I'm driving a car (illegally) I'm always going to have trouble because when I get to a sign, I can't tell what it says. I will always run into that problem and it will always be an obstacle. No situation is completely hopeless. Similarly, there is no situation, no matter how hard we prepare and plan, that is going to be perfect.

In my TEDx Talk "The Gift of Adversity," I mention the same three questions that I asked earlier in the book.

1. If you woke up tomorrow paralyzed from the neck down, what would you wish you would have accomplished with your life?

2. What regrets would you harbor?

3. If by some miracle you were able to walk again, how would you live your life differently?

I do not ask these questions for shock value; I ask them to give both audience and reader an immediate frame of perspective.

Many in life are looking for perspective, even though they lack the perspective to be aware of it. This lack of perspective is what causes midlife crises. This same lack of perspective is even causing quarter-life crises in Millennials, and it's becoming more common by the day.

Without a firm grasp on perspective, we go around fumbling for it clumsily with no resolve. Like the saying goes, it's impossible to see the forest from the trees, yet many keep stumbling through the forest looking for this fabled point of view nonetheless.

Perspective grants us clarity, self-knowledge, and peace. Perspective will always reveal the truth. While hindsight is 20/20, you can't live your entire life looking in the rear-view mirror, and hindsight is always the most ironic point of view.

My injury gave me a tremendous amount of perspective, even though I wasn't looking for it at the time. In my injured state, I was forced to see things differently, because I had no other choice.

There's absolutely no other way I'd have taken as much time to gain this perspective by my own choosing, yet because of it, I am stronger today.

Perspective is the reason someone can ask you to hand them a stapler on the messy desk in front of you, and you can't even see it. Then they walk over and say, "How could you miss it, it was right in front of you? If it were a snake, it would've bit you!" From your perspective, it's hard to see, but from a far enough distance, it can be seen with ease.

That's why it's easy to see when a friend is in a bad relationship. If you are not the one in the relationship, it's easier to see "the big picture." When we don't have emotion hindering our point of view, it's easy to see the flaws and areas that need improvement.

There is a simple thought exercise that can be done to gain perspective for ourselves, in nearly any situation if we are willing to do so. To give yourself the best advice, act as if you are a noninvolved third party. In other words, imagine a friend was describing your current situation or problem to you as their problem. Think of the advice you would give to remedy the situation. Then see if you can take your own advice. In many difficult situations, we often already know what needs to be done. We just don't want to do it.

One Thousand Perspectives in a Minute

While training in the Squad Designated Marksman course, I learned a simple technique that changed how I looked at everything. The exercise was designed to help find targets of opportunity as well as potential threats while deployed. One hundred meters in front of us were a couple of buildings. Behind them was a large tree line.

From the prone position using binoculars, we were to scan the scene looking for everyday military items (an M4 magazine, Gerber multitool, notepad, etc.) that had been hidden. We were given one minute to write down as many items as we could find.

We were then instructed to repeat the exercise, but this time instead of looking as we all had before, from left to right, we were instructed to look from right to left. This simple change in perspective forced us to look at things much more slowly and deliberately. This painstaking perspective made things suddenly leap out that were effectively invisible before. Using this technique, I more than doubled the number of items I found previously.

The concept of looking at the same thing from a different point of view opened my eyes. Take the following sentence as an example: Chuck punched Alex. Now, if we read it a second time from right to left: Alex punched Chuck. The change in context and perspective changes the sentence entirely, especially for Chuck.

Here's the take away: If I show you one perspective, you see but one point of view, but if I teach you an overall concept, you see one thousand perspectives. Understanding something specific gives one perspective, understanding a concept gives you a much higher-level overview. When I teach about an overall concept, I'm trying to show how to think, not what to think. I'm trying to show a way, not the only way. This is how I create and proliferate evergreen ideas and concepts to a new generation of thinking.

This is one of my biggest points I want to make: to give the most poignant lessons I've learned and relearned from my injury, by changing how you view things in your life. These newly discovered views then lead to action.

Perspective of Problem-solving

I could go through and take all the pithy quotes and one-liners that you see on social media and then give you a big collection of them, but in doing so, I wouldn't be true to myself.

Here's a question: what happens when you run into a problem that isn't easily answered by a nicely phrased quote? Will you have the time, money, and desire to comb through every book, both old and new, that covers the subject? This would take up a tremendous amount of precious productivity, time and mental energy to do so.

Here's the follow-up question: What if there isn't a book out there about your specific problem? In business as well as life, we run into problems we've never experienced before. We can ask others for help or Google it, but often, we must figure it out on our own. It is this problem solving that helps us grow. It is this resourcefulness that breeds self-confidence and resilience in the long run.

I'm showing you the art of how to think, understand, and apply the key concepts and principles. I'm not teaching; I'm simply assisting in your own discovery. The goal is to instill in you the fundamental principles and "big ideas" so that you can figure things out on your own without having to have a specific individual answer for every single question that crops up in your journey to success. An overall concept will help you fill in the blanks of your specific problem. You can then plug-in any question that you have and get an answer for your unique situation. This gives you a method of problem-solving for nearly any question that arises.

Some will say that anything you learn is "just another tool in your toolbox," but I've found that if I have a bunch of unnecessary tools in the toolbox, it gets too heavy to carry around, metaphorically. Having more tools than necessary just adds to the problem. Instead, I'm giving you one multi-tool that helps you to figure things out without having to buy a new tool every time something seemingly unique or difficult comes into your life.

It's easy to chase your tail feeling productive by accomplishing things that mean very little in the long run. In the end, it's about not only what we accomplished but also about making sure the things we accomplish are moving us in the right direction. By avoiding the inefficient things, the correct things are done by default.

To reach our goals as efficiently as possible, we don't have the luxury of wasted time and needless actions. Instead, employ simple, direct movements to the most common scenarios so that one answer solves multiple problems in one fell swoop. This decision making makes it that much easier. Hick's Law and 80/20 principle are all great examples of this kind of efficiency. Think of it as a way of sharpening Occam's Razor.

The Crutch

With that said, I utilize massive definitive action with aggressive patience in areas I can control and provide influence. These coupled mindsets keep me focused while simultaneously letting me press ever onward towards my objective.

I employ a Stoic and Taoist mentality regarding situations that I cannot control. These philosophies help me tolerate the temporary hardship while remaining focused on the overall long-term goal. They remind me that if it's something that can't be controlled, then it simply must be endured, and will eventually pass. I cannot control the rain, but I can control how I feel as I'm getting wet.

However, and I cannot stress this enough, DO NOT use these or ANY philosophy as a crutch! These are not self-defeated mentalities. Instead, see these as ways to endure the not-so-pleasant trials requisite to succeed. No matter your decision, you must realize that there is a philosophical reinforcement for it. Regardless of the justification you may or may not come up with, you can find a person, thought process, or ideology that will support it. The people that no longer have the will and have given up, are now afforded these philosophical luxuries because so many others have done so before them. To avoid this fate, we must employee brutal honestly to look closely and see the truth of the situation. In other words, know your worth. Not just your own, but the value of the things you desire to achieve.

You know how willing you are to work for the things you want because you know what they mean to you. Don't fall back on some bullshit saying to justify your weakness. Don't let the fact that you are gutless be the act of subterfuge that allows weak-mindedness.

People don't respect what they don't pay for. That's why if it were easy or free, you wouldn't value it. Pay the price. Don't let the fact that you're not willing to go down without a fight afford you the opportunity to quit. Don't be a mere shell of what you could've been by choosing the path of mediocrity. If you choose the philosophical crutch to justify your behavior, then you are aware of that truth. You understand that you are choosing to be weak.

Remember that when you say, "I can't" you are saying, "I'm willfully choosing convenience over happiness." But don't worry, you'll be surrounded by millions of other mediocre people that are taking the same path of least resistance, and they will be happy to have you in their fold, opening their arms wide to bring you in to coddle you. "There, there, it's okay that you didn't succeed," they will tell you. "Hey, it's not so bad, we did the same thing! Go ahead give up on all the things you thought were important, give up your dreams. You'll forget all about it before you know it with enough distraction!"

I hope that the mere thought of that conformity makes you sick to your stomach. I hope it makes you feel disgusted with yourself for even thinking of compromising, to accept something less than what you're worthy of. If it doesn't sicken you, then you have already made your decision and you are already there; you just don't yet see the new boundaries that now surround you.

Success or Failure?

Success or failure? It's all relative. Therefore, success is relative. One man's huge success can represent another man's complete and utter failure.

I don't play poker for the money, although it's nice. I do it for entertainment as well as the mental and intellectual stimulation of playing the game. Yes, I know that sounds like an oxymoron because if you've ever been at a poker table at 3 A.M. in Las Vegas, you know that a high degree of intellect is not usually on display. On one such night, I saw a man at one of the higher limit poker tables. And he was absolutely crushing it.

I was playing at a lower limit table while this player was seated a few feet away at the table in front of me, perfectly in my field of view. As the night wore on, I would watch him when I wasn't involved in a hand. I was very impressed.

In every way, he appeared the consummate poker player. He developed a read on the other players accurately, could sniff out bluffs and calculated pot odds smoothly and precisely. He appeared to be putting on a clinic. It seemed like every time I looked up, he was dragging in larger and larger pots. As I was taking a break from the table to walk around and wake up a bit, I saw him walking towards the cage to cash out. While it's rude to stare at the amount of money a player is carrying, he looked to have more than $100,000 in his stack. I looked at him and said, "not a bad night?"

The player looked at me, then his chips. "Oh THIS?" he said pointing to his winnings. He then started laughing as if he'd heard the funniest joke in his life. "Well, when you consider I've lost nearly a million in the last 24 hours, this isn't very good at all!" You can imagine my surprise. This player, who I'd witnessed commanding the table for the last few hours, had lost almost $1,000,000 in the last 24 hours?!

Success and failure, it all comes down to perspective.

From my perspective, he had an incredibly successful session, but from his, it was a tremendous failure compared to how much he had lost previously. This is precisely why some do not think of actions in terms of success or failure but simply, results and experiences. This reinforces the "I either win or I learn" mentality, and time and experience are the best creators of perspective.

"You never know how far reaching something you think, say or do today, will affect the lives of millions tomorrow."

-Dr. B.J. Palmer-

If you've ever been in any kind of need before in your life, you understand how incredible a kind act from a stranger can be. When you need help, that act of kindness means the world. A simple act that takes very little effort on your part can make someone's day.

As I was parking my car, I saw a woman getting into hers. As she was shutting the door, her cell phone fell on the ground. I quickly picked it up and ran to get her attention before she drove off. By simply being observant, I returned her phone before she even realized she'd lost it. As you can imagine she was incredibly grateful. "This phone is my life! Thank you, thank you, thank you!" was her reply. While that small act didn't change the world, it certainly changed her world for the better. This ripple effect is very powerful. It's powerful because it creates momentum that builds on itself. Realize that a simple act of kindness costs us little, but may mean the world to someone else. Without much effort, you can easily buy someone food, help them with some work on a project, or spend a small amount of time with them when they are in need of quality company. It pays huge dividends not only for you but for them as well. It is the very definition of a win-win scenario. While the money and time spent may not seem like much to you, that magnanimous act and gesture could mean the world to them. I guarantee you won't miss money you spent helping them in comparison to the impact you had on that person's life, and that gesture will be with them as long as they walk this earth.

While on a date in a nice restaurant one cold evening, I noticed a man had wandered in and sat at a table. He looked disheveled and a little confused. Still holding a conversation with my date, I could see from the man's attire that he was likely homeless. As the server approached him, the man said loudly that he just wanted water, then started asking if the bread was free. The server informed him that it was free with his meal, but he'd have to buy a meal for the complimentary bread. The man then asked what the cheapest thing on the menu was, to which the server replied, "the hamburger." The man asked about the price of the salmon, and the server told him it was the market price. The man said he'd think about it, but to go ahead and bring the bread. I then saw the man start to pull out loose change and a few crumpled up $1 bills, well short of the price of even a hamburger in this establishment.

I excused myself from the table and went to talk to the now perturbed waiter as he passed, telling him to put an order of salmon, as well as a hamburger and anything else the man ordered to eat on my tab, just not to let the man know who paid for it. The server was incredibly relieved. The look on the man's face when all the food showed up at his table was worth every penny. Before the man could even say anything, the server told him that it had been paid for by a Good Samaritan. I kept my eyes on my date as the man looked around the restaurant trying to figure out who had sent the meal, but his gaze never rested on me. As I got the check, the server said the man looked like he was about to cry with happiness. I have no idea how long he had gone without food, but at least for tonight, I knew that man wouldn't be hungry or embarrassed for wanting to come in from the cold and have a hot meal. I tipped the waiter handsomely with the man and my date none the wiser of my act.

To echo Dr. Palmer's earlier quote, you never know how far reaching a good deed may go. I don't know how close to his wits end that homeless man in the restaurant may have been. Who knows, maybe my simple act, while it took little for me to do, may have been the difference between life and death for him. That simple act may have been the one shred of human decency that he needed to experience to give him hope.

Sometimes the simplest act of one person can be the sign that another's been waiting their entire lives for. To one person, it may mean nothing, but to another it means destiny.

Of course, what one person considers to be kindness and courtesy can seem like overt oppression to another.

Courteous or Oppression?

One cold Kansas City morning, I was running my errands for the day. Going to the bank was my first stop. As I approached the door of the bank, I could see a person in a heavy winter coat and hat walking not far behind me in the window's reflection. Having common situational awareness, I opened the door to let them enter first. As I turned and faced the person, who happened to be a woman, she stopped walking.

She looked at me, then the door, then back at me. The look on her face was a mixture of someone who had heard their least favorite song from their least favorite genre by that genre's worst performer at loud volume, combined with the look of a person who had just smelled something horrible. As you can imagine, this wasn't exactly the reaction I was expecting from my act of civility.

As I continued to hold the door, waiting for her to walk through, she began to speak, but her body language was loud and clear before ever she opened her mouth. "Do you know that when you hold the door open for me, you deny me the opportunity to open the door for myself? That by holding the door, you are TAKING my power from me?" I stood, still holding the door, in stunned silence. I was beyond flabbergasted.

She continued, "Let me ask you a question, would you have opened the door for me if I were a man?" After finally getting my bearings, I responded, "I would have opened the door regardless of your gender. I just considered it common courtesy."

Unfazed she replied, "Well, I wouldn't have opened it for you." I paused then said, "I guess what I consider common courtesy, you do not."

Full disclosure, I was not trying to flirt or go out of my way to talk to this person. I couldn't even tell the sex of the person because of the heavy jacket and limited point of view I had from the door's reflection. I was simply trying to be courteous, which can obviously be misconstrued by others.

Finally, I said, "I apologize if I offended you" and entered the building. The woman waited for both pairs of doors to close completely before she decided to enter a few moments after I did.

Was mine an act of courteous or oppression? Clearly, I had no ill intent in my actions. I replayed the interaction in my mind after I left the bank. At first, I was offended by her reaction, but then I tried to see the incident through her eyes. Perhaps she had reason to be overly cautious. For example, she may have been victimized by someone in a similar situation before. Maybe she thought I looked intimidating in some manner. Perhaps she was just ferociously independent. Again, I have no real way of knowing. So, instead of being upset or offended, I felt at peace. Taking just a moment to see things from her potential point of view helped me realize that I can't control the actions of others, I can only control my own.

We should never take anything anybody says or does to heart. Be it good or bad, complementary or derogatory, if you know who you are as a person, you will not allow something insignificant illicit a response. Never allow the number of 'likes' you get on a post or negative comment on another change your vision. This also grants resolve if someone tries to criticize in a not so constructive manner.

Another's opinion about you does not make it so. Use this logic if someone claims you are something that you know is false. Having steadfast knowledge of yourself allows you to stay strong in your convictions. This leads to staying strong in your intent and actions. Again, it all depends on your perspective. And perspective will dictate truth in the eye of the beholder.

"No man ever steps in the same river twice. For it's not the same river, and he's not the same man."

-Heraclitus-

I love reading a good book again a couple of years later. It's amazing how many new things you can pick up from the second, or even third reading. There are many books that I read once a year for this reason. Conversely, there are books that I've loved in the past that no longer have the impact they once did.

So, what's different now? Obviously, the book hasn't changed, the reader has. It's funny now that I'm a bit wiser, I can better understand parts of books that were lost on me the first few times I read them. I didn't see the wisdom in them the first or second read because I wasn't wise enough to recognize it. I hope that the evergreen content in this book will be something you can continue to read, learn from and enjoy for years to come as well.

Perspective Travel

We should all travel more. Going to a far-off land or even to another city that you've never explored 200 miles away shifts our minds into adventure mode. This perspective makes us think of all the possibilities that such a trek can create. We gain perspective when we are forced out of our normal environments. I've had epiphanies everywhere I've traveled from Rome to South Africa, from the French Rivera to The Dominican Republic, experiencing moments of almost Zen-like revelation.

Travel to some may seem a hassle and daunting but think of any book you've ever read that had a hero in it. The hero is given a task that must be undertaken, and it always involves a journey physically or emotionally. Having this sort of mentality and being open to discovery is what makes the adventure worth the effort.

Being a stranger in a strange land forces us to stretch our thinking in ways we wouldn't normally, inviting new thought patterns and neurological pathways. These excursions create the distance that allows a crystal-clear perspective of what is happening in our lives at that moment in time. Often the answers we've been searching for becoming readily apparent in these new environments.

When we travel to another country, it's invigorating. The language and music are exotic and different. The smells and sights are foreign and new, causing our senses to expand and contract to find equilibrium. By being in an unfamiliar place, we have no choice but to do things differently and to step out of our comfort zones. The food, weather, and people help us see the uniqueness of the surrounding culture while observing the common thread of human nature regardless of the language or altitude of air you inspire.

Experiencing new cultures (and potentially having an internet and social media holiday) helps our bodies and mind re-engage in the human interaction that some have lost sight of or never knew existed. This lets us rediscover simple joy of human interaction. Even having a bit of deja-vu while traveling is an exciting experience. It shows us that the world isn't as large a place as previously believed and that we as people aren't quite as different as we may have previously thought. The person you were when you embark on your journey is never the same person that returns. The emotions, experiences, and encounters you have will change you in some small way, creating depth within you as a person.

After your journey has concluded and you return home, you will look at things a little differently. The trip will offer perspective, and with it, appreciation of the things you've missed. The creature comforts, familiar sounds, and smells will help you feel relief from your travels; but, the lingering feeling held over from being on your trek can create a longing for your previous adventure. Even if the trip was difficult and trying, rest assured there will be some memory or experience that you will reflect on. It could be something as simple as smelling the rainfall, seeing something in nature, or a smile from a stranger on this adventure. In that moment of reflection, you will smile and perhaps even laugh to yourself silently.

That moment, whatever it may be to you, is the reason travel is an adventure. That is an experience you could never buy and that you could never have had unless you went on this trip. It's moments like this that give us renewed confidence in our current domicile. After dealing with the stress of figuring our every move you will make while on holiday, falling back into the same routine of home feels like putting on your favorite pair of jeans; comfortable, well-worn, and familiar. After your trip when confronted with a slight curve ball in your day-to-day life, you'll respond to it with more authority and conviction because compared to your travels, this inconvenience isn't even an issue.

There are still many places I want to explore and experiences I want to taste. I want to evolve with every breath I take. Even now, I've never regretted any of the jobs or experiences I've had.

Yes, even including my injuries. All those small steps, even in the wrong direction, have led me here to this moment in time, and if I'd changed even a millimeter of my path, then my journey would've been different, and this book would never have been written.

Chapter X

Thirsty

"It is impossible for a man to learn what he thinks he already knows."

- Seneca -

A professor of philosophy came seeking an audience with the oldest living Zen master in Japan. After the formal introductions and pleasantries were exchanged, they sat down and the professor started talking...and talking, and talking, he would not shut his mouth. The professor droned on and on about the countless papers he had written on Zen that had been published, the doctorate he was awarded because of his research of Zen, how he was teaching the subject at a highly esteemed university, and that because of these things, he was considered the "Zen expert" in the West. This went on for several agonizing minutes.

All the while sitting in silence listening patiently, the Zen master eventually gestured towards the teapot on the table to inquire if the professor would like a cup. Still talking, the professor nodded his head enthusiastically as he continued to 'enlighten' the Zen master, a man who had been practicing Zen nearly twice as long as the chatty professor had been alive and gulping air on this earth.

The old master put an empty cup before the professor and slowly began to pour the tea. As the professor continued to pontificate, the master continued to fill the cup. He poured until the cup was full, then kept pouring some more. He poured until the cup overflowed, running over onto the table and eventually onto the professor's trousers causing him to exclaim, "Stop pouring! Can't you see the cup is full and can hold no more?!"

The Zen master finally stopped. His knowing eyes fell on the professor, his face giving a wrinkled smile as he watched the academic who was still clearly flustered by the demonstration. The master said in a clear and ancient tone, "You are like this teacup; full of your own ideas about what Zen is. How can I possibly teach you anything if you are already full? If you want to learn, you must first empty your cup."

Empty Your Cup

Variations of this classic Zen tale have been told probably for centuries, but in our current age of information saturation, the message is even truer today. To "empty your cup" doesn't mean that you get rid of everything you have ever learned and fallen back into ignorance. It simply means to have an open mind about a subject and be humble and willing to learn. While we always try to increase the size of our "cup" (our capacity to learn) it's still very easy to become enamored by our own experiences and opinions causing our cup to overflow, disallowing more knowledge to be gained.

To empty your cup, you must first stop pouring into it. Eventually you come to a point in your development where your influx of knowledge reaches its limit and you must put the knowledge you've already gathered into action, otherwise, it becomes watered down, lost, or even forgotten. I agree that having a steady stream of new information is good for keeping intellectually stimulated. However, if you genuinely want to assimilate any of the material that you are taking in, you must take the time to digest it. Absorbing something new requires consistent and diligent effort and reinforcement. Therefore, take your time and be selective about what you want to learn. Be certain that it's something worthy of your time. Once this new knowledge has been successfully ingrained, it's much easier to use when needed.

If you are not implementing this new information, regardless of how precious it may be, it is still just an act of intellectual subterfuge on your part. I understand that there are some things that can be taken conceptually or philosophically and implemented with little effort (being positive, being grateful, being present, etc.) but there are other things that require a tremendous amount of time and energy to gain the benefit from and these are things of which I speak.

You may have just returned from a mind-blowing seminar, or perhaps you saw a life-changing personal development speaker. From this, you may have learned the most revolutionary and transformational knowledge ever bestowed upon you. It may even be the truth you've been searching your entire life for. Filled with new motivation, you go to the bookstore and buy half a dozen books on the subject from their recommendations. You also purchase an online program as well as a few more books.

But stop for a second, step back and take a deep breath. Much like a child going to a buffet for the first time, with so many things looking appealing and tantalizing, it's very tempting to want to devour everything in sight. We all know what happens when our eyes get too big for our stomach; we feel miserable and possibly even get sick. Why? Because we are unable to digest everything that we are consuming.

If you are unable or simply too mentally overwhelmed by the sheer volume of information you have taken in to know where to begin, regardless of how life-changing and useful, it is still utterly useless. The lesson is to master the skills and concepts you want to acquire currently, instead of constantly looking for the 'newest thing' to somehow magically complete your shortcomings.

Be honest with yourself and realize that you will have to program these newly learned ideas and principles into habits. You are learning something new, and newly acquired information takes time to absorb fully. This teaches us to be very selective about the things that we are trying to put into our thought processes and routine. It's incredibly important to weigh the pros and cons to see if the result will be worth the time and effort required to use it effectively.

If you decided to start a new diet, an intense workout schedule, begin meditating for 20 minutes twice a day all within the same week of starting a new job, it would be difficult to give any of those new activities the attention they deserve to be useful to you in the long run. By even attempting and then inevitably failing to be able to maintain them exposes you to unnecessary stress, self-judgment, and discouragement. However, if you'd waited until after you'd acclimated to the new job and then introduced these new habits one at a time, there's a much better chance of sticking to them.

Of course, you don't stop learning. But eventually, you realize that reading a book (or buying a handful of books with the intention of reading, but never getting around to finishing) won't get you any closer to your goal. You realize that MORE information will not change anything, at least not for the better. If anything, a greater stream of knowledge will confuse more than clarify.

Realize that you must make the knowledge you currently possess actionable. You must act on the knowledge that you've already gathered. Understand that if you read a book and learn some new idea or principle that it will take some time to put it into motion in your own life and make it stick. It will take consistent practice and repetition to start using it on a regular basis.

It's useless to read hundreds of books if you can't implement or even recall anything you've read or learned. It is the repetition that creates the mastery of any skill, and having a bunch of ideas in your head that you cannot put into action does little to forward your journey to success. It would do little good to read the greatest books ever written and hear the most inspirational speeches of all time if we put none of it into action. We must put into practice these skills and philosophies to improve. Rarely does anything good in life happens passively as if by osmosis, that's a false promise somebody tells to get you to buy something.

The reality is we must apply our efforts to legitimately "own" the most important knowledge that will guide and last a lifetime, and that's a small price to pay when you think about it. The same way a sword won't protect you by simply having it in your possession, having knowledge while being unable or unwilling to apply it does nothing to make it come to fruition. What we know is worthless, we are what you do consistently. The information in this book is no different. Knowledge is the equivalent of ignorance when not put into action. Instead of reading (or intending to read) every new book that comes out, there is an easier way to get more out of what you are learning. The more efficient idea is to find the commonalities of all the information you are reading and learning about and then put those similar lessons into play.

For example, if you read six different books on productivity and they ALL mention the need to reduce distraction when you're working, then that should be a big indicator that you need to do everything in your power to reduce distraction.

Look for the common concepts in everything you learn. Once you understand the overarching idea, you'll be amazed at how many places you'll find this newly learned concept in your everyday life.

Enlightened

"The truth is anyone can repeat wise words, but to truly appreciate wisdom takes life experience."

-Marcus Aurelius Anderson-

Some philosophies speak of a moment of clarity or "enlightenment." This is a moment when everything falls into place and becomes clear. These moments of lucidity can occur in times of complete chaos or during moments of quiet tranquility, sometimes one creating the other. They make it sound as if once someone has become enlightened that everything else in life is simple and easy. It's romanticized as if it's all rainbows, butterflies, and unicorns from then on, THE END, roll credits, please.

But that's not exactly how it works. It's important to understand that being "enlightened" is fine, but if you return to your previous behavior and mentality, then your enlightenment was short lived at best. It does no good to learn a lesson only to stop putting it into practice or to have it forgotten completely.

Yes, we gain wisdom from our own experiences as well as absorbing lessons from others we trust enough to listen to and learn from. Even if we learn something that is truly life-changing, something that would truly "enlighten," it would be worthless if it's not continually practiced.

In other words, once enlightened we should always try to stay in sight of it. What good is it to have this magnificent clarity only to let it fade away? Like being reminded of an important lesson that we have overlooked or forgotten, putting wisdom into action again is what helps us rediscover it's significant.

I realize now that my Adversity was the very thing I needed in my life to grant my "enlightenment." Adversity is a gift, but it's more than that, it's also a huge responsibility. However, there's something that needs to be said, and it's something that will probably come as a bit of a surprise.

And Yet...

Let me reiterate how incredibly grateful I am every day to be given a second chance at life.

I try to do everything in my power to live this life to the fullest. I understand how fortunate I am to be able to have such an opportunity. This second chance has let me taste tremendous success in many endeavors that I have been working so diligently towards. And yet, after all that I've learned and been through from my experience, there are days when I still struggle.

Even now, there are times when I may be momentarily tempted to slack and ask lesser of myself. It still takes hard work and dedication to stay the course to achieve the goals that I have set for me. While success breeds more success, it can also breed something else: complacency. Complacency is the kiss of death of ambition.

Even though I've been enlightened by my Adversity, life still has its difficulties. I say this to show that even though the Gift of Adversity has shown me my potential and set my wildest ambitions in motion, I must still push myself every day to use my time to the best of my ability and stay focused on my priorities. It's an ever-ongoing process to continually exceed my previous best.

I'm very grateful for the emails and messages I get from people who have been positively influenced by my story and work. I'm thankful for every podcast interview as well as TV and radio show I've had the honor of being on. I cannot put into words how blown away I am when I shake someone's hand and they tell me that I've changed their life for the better. Being told that my words are the very thing that stopped a person from potentially taking their own life and bringing them out of the darkness of depression is humbling. These results are the reason I embarked on this journey in the first place.

Now that I've been given a glimpse of what I am capable, I feel a tremendous obligation not only to myself but to countless others, to accomplish everything that I've envisioned. To leave these things undone after all I've discovered about myself would be a colossal travesty.

I've mentioned previously that Adversity is relative to each person. I've also come to realize that Adversity is very much about proximity. Once we've gone through something difficult and traumatic, the natural tendency is to mentally put as much distance between ourselves and that place as possible. We want to push it out of our mind and bury it as a defense mechanism to protect us from the pain, and this is completely normal. But hear me out. This time of pain and discomfort is a rare opportunity that we should use to our advantage, and like all Adversity, it's very difficult to have this mindset while we are going through the most difficult part of this tribulation.

Our recent pain and hardship is the gateway to a better understanding of ourselves. This creates a state that is open and raw, and though painful, it is the best time to examine the motivations of our thoughts and fears. It is always best to do this while it's fresh in our mind and emotions.

Truthfully, what we fear is not the pain; we fear what the pain may reveal. We are afraid that we may find out things about ourselves that we are not at all proud of. We fear it will reveal shortcomings, remind us of lost ambitions, and moments of weakness that have lasted a lifetime. It is imperative to remember that these imperfections are what make us human, and regardless of how hard we try to avoid these times of discomfort, it's still a part of us that we need to keep sight of.

The things that we aren't proud of are the very things we should explore. Only after examining these things will we be able to eventually accept them as a part of us, and to accept these things without judgment is necessary. Only then will we have a chance to potentially improve on these shortcomings. Even if we are unable to change them, accepting them is what is necessary to be able to co-exist with them healthily. This precious knowledge reveals an inner truth, giving us the bearings needed to find direction. This self-acceptance creates peace of mind, which lets everything in our lives flow without inhibition.

To live without inhibition is the ultimate form of freedom. Because of this, I choose to keep some form of Adversity close at hand. By giving myself small, "micro Adversities" I keep this mindset fresh to apply it elsewhere in life. These "micro Adversities" can be as simple as fasting, taking the stairs instead of the elevator, or delaying pleasure in any number of ways to prove to myself that I can endure more than I'd previously anticipated.

These things serve as a reminder of the previous mental complacency and self-chosen mediocrity I exhibited before my injury, my moment of clarity. I am forever grateful for where I am currently, but this has created an urgency in me that I never knew existed. Like I've mentioned before, the unique knowledge gained from my injury and recovery is worthless unless put into action.

Re-learn

Everyone seems to be waiting on something. They seem to be waiting for "this" or "that" to happen. They think that once they have this material possession or when that event to occurs, then they'll begin to act on their plan. Many seem to be searching for that one magical nugget of information that they haven't found to make them happy and successful. I was doing the same thing before my accident.

I ask you now, what is it that you currently lack that's preventing you from achieving the things you truly desire in life? Chances are you don't lack food, shelter, and clothing. What are you waiting for? Most of the things we lack are not material or monetary, they are the things that are currently within our reach, but we haven't acted on for one reason or another.

The reality is, you already possess what you need to be happy and successful now, and you need to start putting in the effort to make it happen. From engaging in a stronger work ethic to spending more quality time with the people that mean the most to you in your life, these are things that money won't buy.

It won't happen overnight and it won't be easy. In fact, the greater the goal you seek, the harder the path to achieving it, but the greatness in success lies in overcoming the difficulty of the challenge. Time and effort are all that is needed to achieve anything you want in life, and both of those things are under your control.

Success is about executing on the knowledge that is in your possession at this moment. Instead of trying to accumulate a bunch of other knowledge that leads in a million different directions, focus on what you can accomplish with the knowledge you currently have. You will learn that the most valuable information comes from doing, the most useful knowledge comes from our own experiences.

Learning

Learning lessons are great, but being able to remember to put them into practice is what's most important. I have found that even when I review something that I've learned before, I am often reminded of something that I had already learned but lost sight of. I am constantly learning and relearning lessons all the time.

The more experiences you have in life, the more knowledge you will genuinely possess. The more you learn, the more knowledge you will be able to gain in the future. Like learning a language, if you don't learn fundamental words and phrases, you'll never become fluent enough to understand and express yourself in this foreign tongue. The knowledge that you possess now is the building block for what you will be able to learn in the future. If you don't try to learn new things and push yourself, you'll be stuck in your current level of understanding, which means you'll be unable to recognize potential opportunities in the future. Even if you are presented with an amazing opportunity, it will look like and sound like gibberish if you can't understand the language.

There are many stages of learning. We spend much of our time in the initial stage learning many lessons, some more important than others. The next stage, we learn which lessons to let go of. Finally, when we reach the point of equilibrium and wisdom, we relearn the lessons that were precious but forgotten. It is the lessons we take the time to value enough to relearn from which we learn the most. It's also important to realize that in many ways, enlightenment is simply the act of letting go of that which no longer serves you. The path to learning can seem long and arduous. When we are impatient and fatigued it's natural to look for shortcuts.

The reason some will try to shortcut something is because they don't see the significance of the task they are trying to accomplish, because they don't value it, they don't care enough to put in the effort to do it to the best of their ability. But, here's the thing. The long way is the shortcut. Although it seems to take a lot of effort at the time, it takes much less time and effort than doing it poorly and having to come back to do it correctly again later. The reality is that if it is something that needs to be done, it needs to be done to the best of our ability to save time and effort later.

This comes back to Priorities. If you've done the work to decide on the things you genuinely desire and mapped out a game plan to succeed, then every single step in that plan must be handled with the same attention to detail and care that you'd exercise as if it were the last task between you and the achievement of your goal. It is important to realize that all the "big, important things" in life are made up of many small things. Only when these smaller things are done correctly and then brought carefully together can we achieve the larger objective that we have in mind. In other words, if you care about it, you'll do every bit of it correctly.

If you find yourself in an occupation or situation where you don't care about doing a good job, then that's your fault. Yes, your fault. It's your fault because ultimately you are the one who decides what you do from day to day. If you don't like your job, then it's up to you start looking for one you will like. This is one of the main reasons entrepreneurs start their own business.

Work Ethic vs. Race to Burn Out

"If you think adventure is dangerous, try routine, it is lethal."

-Paulo Coelho-

Many who have an "entrepreneurial spirit" today are very proud of their work ethic and hustle. There are many entrepreneurs who just keep working frantically because they have a "fast cash" mentality. They want to make as much money in the shortest time possible so they can retire by age 25 instead of having a purpose driven vision that cares about the product or service created for a customer that is valued and respected. This is a one-way ticket to burning out. I've seen this happen time and again in multiple businesses and professions, which is why I do everything in my power to avoid it.

I have created a business from my experiences, expertise, and passions. For me, there is never an urgency to "retire" because I truly enjoy what I do so much. I can't put into words how gratifying it is to help people uncover their strength and potential. This incredible positive feedback I receive keeps me ever focused.

My vision of purpose pulls me onward. The more I help others, the more I learn. And the more I learn, the better I can help others, and so the cycle is never-ending.

It seems that some of the more popular CEO's and entrepreneurs right now are permanently in an almost obsessive and unhealthy work mode. They're positively consumed by it. Some even speak of how they more than willingly give up quality time with their family and kids regularly just to keep up with their "grind."

If they heard my disagreement, I'm sure they would have some comment along the lines of "oh yeah, what's your net worth Adversity guru?" or "well it's not my fault that you can't grind as hard as I do, I'm a machine!" etc. While I may not have as much money as they do, I don't want it. At least, not for the price that they are willing to pay to gain it.

In previous chapters, I've written about how people will work a horrible 9-5 job for money despite how much they utterly hate it. I go on to show that trying to justify a job that pays an extra $10-20,000 a year is a thin excuse indeed. Working the extra hours, enduring the omnipresent stress and having it affect your family and home life negatively for a few hundred extra dollars a week is a waste in my mind. I feel the same way about giving up your time, experiences, and possibly health for the sake of money, especially if you already have as much of it as these people claim to possess. And for those who don't agree with me, that's fine. Mine is just one man's opinion.

Do I work hard? Of course. Am I motivated? Absolutely. Are there times when I must work frantically to meet my own self-imposed deadlines? I do, but not for long, unhealthy periods of time.

I am simply true to myself and my nature by doing what I'm made to do. To me, there is no competition where money is the means to keep score. Some popular entrepreneurs have even said that the grind is "their drug." This shows their priorities. And I agree that if giving up "the grind" makes them miserable then they should absolutely continue to do so.

However, a happy, healthy, and fulfilled life is about balance. I want to be able to enjoy the fruits of my labor with friends and family. It makes no sense to slowly kill myself for money because when you're dead, you can't take it with you. Believe me, I've thought long and hard about this.

As for the idea that your family will get the money and legacy you've created, I ask you this: would your family rather have the money and legacy you leave behind or would they simply wish to have you live with them for a longer period of quality of time to create beautiful memories? Let that answer lead you.

Another thing people don't seem to talk as much about is the amount of depression by those trying to chase this alleged "entrepreneurial easy money lifestyle" that is perpetuated on social media. Having money and success does no good if you aren't mentally healthy enough to even enjoy it.

The Value of Physical and Mental Health

This should go without saying, but I'm saying it; we take our health for granted. I know that I certainly did. Yes, it sounds cliché, but that doesn't stop it from being true.

For better or worse, many value money more than they do their health. If forced to choose between seeing the doctor or getting their car fixed, most will choose to fix the car. This is because when a person is young and healthy, they have more health than money. As time wears on, things take a turn and go the opposite direction, often sooner than hoped or expected. The answer to staying healthy is prevention. This makes exercise, diet, rest, and stress reduction the cornerstones of health.

We don't realize how much we take our health for granted until we no longer have it. We take our eyesight for granted until we must squint to read something for the first time, our flexibility for granted until we pull a hamstring playing a friendly game of basketball, and our strength for granted until we hurt our back trying to pick something up off the floor.

Many of the revelations I've had since my experience will be universal, but they will resonate on different levels for different people at different times in their lives. Even so, hopefully the words I've written will uncover a feeling or idea that will strike a chord with you. The goal is to help you ask the correct questions of yourself and your life to find the answers and desires you never knew existed or perhaps have forgotten about.

For example, perhaps you would've wished to spend more quality time with your children. Playing catch or going for a walk in the spring with your children may be an activity that is long overdue. Showing your undying love and admiration for your significant other may be something that you'd wished you'd done more of, so do it now while you are still alive and able. Telling your parents, family, and close friends how much they mean to you and reflecting on these relationships and the positive impact they've made on your life is something that should be done sooner than later.

In the end, it's about being happy, satisfied and fulfilled with your choices in this life. This requires us to slow down and offset the insanity of the long, intense hours. I feel secure and happy in my choices and have no desire to compete in a monetary manner with anyone. If you're doing what makes you feel happy and fulfilled, there's more than enough money to go around. I've had plenty of time to reflect on what is important to me in my life and I have no regrets. I hope this book helps grant the same success coupled with serenity for you as well.

"Keep sharpening your knife

and it will blunt.

Chase after money and security

and your heart will never unclench.

Care about people's approval

and you will be their prisoner."

-Lao Tzu, Tao Te Ching-

After recovering from my injury, I gained a renewed sense of purpose. My motivation was on fire! With this newfound enthusiasm came an unforeseen problem: I had to learn to reign myself back.

As it alludes to in the above Tao Te Ching passage, we can push ourselves very hard, but we also need to give ourselves breaks both physically and mentally. If we do not, we dull the blade. When I was younger, I didn't believe this to be true. I realize only now from hindsight that even back then I was dulling the blade, I was just unable to recognize it. Alas, truth is truth, whether we recognize it or not.

We do our best work consistently when we are well rested and mentally charged. "Hustle" and "grind" are all the rage now, and such buzzwords imply the need for hard work. I agree that hard work is crucial to being successful in anything, but realize that the cumulative effects of physical fatigue and mental burn out are very real. Without allowing time for recovery, all the "hustle" and "grind" in the world amounts to nothing more than a fool's errand in the end.

If we focus on a problem for too long, we start getting stressed out about it. Trying to micromanage every aspect of your life usually creates a tremendous amount of undue stress. Prolonged stress reduces focus, which ultimately decreases productivity. Remember that there is such a thing as diminishing returns. There are times when we can accomplish more by simply doing less. Recognize the times when more can be accomplished by doing nothing. I can go without much food, water, and sleep when necessary, but I've learned from experience that I won't be able to do my best creative work in such a depleted state.

Realize that if you want to improve and progress in something, we must allow time for recovery which allows adaptation. If the fastest you can run a mile is twelve minutes, hoping to run a six-minute mile the following day would be setting yourself up for disappointment. When it comes to long-term success, it's about consistency, not just intensity.

The Power of Ponder

The secret to saving a tremendous amount of time and effort, in the long run, is to take these planned periodic breaks. Because eventually, our mind and body will force us to take a break, one way or another.

The need for rest is unavoidable. Like pushing ourselves until our immune system is completely run down and getting sick, eventually, your body will just force you to stop and remedy the situation. And it always seems to happen during the most inopportune times. It probably occurs more often than you realize.

For instance, you're thinking about a task and before you know it, for the life of you, you can't remember what you were about to do. Or you're lost in thought at the stop light when you hear the horn of the impatient driver blare behind you because the light changed unbeknownst to you.

Don't get angry with yourself about this, the mind does this because it needs to. It would be like getting angry with yourself for falling asleep or being hungry. This is simply a symptom. Instead of being upset at yourself, find the causation. Finding the cause allows us to find the cure. When you find what's really causing this (sleep deprivation, stress, bad food choices, the inability to focus or relax) you can remedy it and other potential problems in one fail swoop if it addressed correctly.

From catching ourselves zoning out and staring off into space to just feeling mentally and physically lethargic, our body and mind will let us know when it needs a break. All the signs are there if we are willing to see them. Our mind does this because it needs to unplug.

Have you noticed that you get some of your best ideas as you're about to nod off to sleep? Why is this?

This happens because it is only during times of silence and peace that we can truly hear what's going on inside our mind. This state of physical rest allows the mind a chance to finally relax and release all the thoughts from the day.

Of course, there is another potential phenomenon that occurs when trying to go to sleep. Our body is exhausted, but for some reason, our mind shifts into overdrive. Our brain is doing mental cartwheels thinking about everything from the tasks that we didn't get done today that now must be done tomorrow, financial and relationship concerns as well as the chorus to that damn song you haven't heard since high school, but is now stuck in your head on infinite repeat for some reason.

Again, this is because the mind is finally able to let go. This mental decompression means that there are all kinds of thoughts that have been bouncing around inside our psyche for days, months or possibly years.

For some, this may be the first time that they've experienced actual silence all day, and silence is devastating when all you're accustomed to is noise. It is during this silence that we can hear our true self, once we've allowed the muddy waters of our mind to settle.

The better option is to take small breaks of our own volition instead of continually pushing ourselves to the point of breaking down. Once we hit this breaking point, it requires twice as much time to recover from.

I apply the concept of periodic rest in many facets of life. Having the 50:10 protocol keeps me focused on my immediate task at hand. I do the same thing with hard physical training cycles, taking at least a week off for every 12 weeks of heavy lifting and hard martial arts training. I apply similar downtime when it comes to business. Many of my projects take months of work to achieve, so having a bit of downtime between projects works out perfectly.

It's fine to relax and let the mind wander. In fact, it's a necessity.

What should you do if you don't have time to take a few days off? Most of us don't have the luxury of being able to take a vacation at a moment's notice, what's the answer then?

Mini-mental vacations.

We gain huge insights from traveling and exploring new places because it causes a physical change in perspective. Meditating is much like giving your mind a temporary vacation from the usual daily demands of life.

These temporary mental vacations are necessary not only to stay productive but to stay sane. Without allow yourself time to relax and reflect, we not only lose sight of where we're going. We lose appreciation for where we've gone before as well as where we come from. This puts us back on the Hedonic Treadmill, which is a terrible place to be.

There are plenty of downloadable apps that can be used to meditate. Even ten minutes once a day can make a huge difference in focus, concentration and stress reduction. But if you aren't into the whole "woo woo" notion conjured from the word meditation, you've probably engaged in some form of meditation whether you realize it or not. There is no need to wear elaborate robes, burn incense, and chant to get the benefits of meditation. Think of meditation simply as a form of focused attention. If you've ever engaged in physical activity or repetitive action that lets you lose yourself in the movement, congratulations you've meditated.

Athletes refer to it as "flow" or "flow state." The Japanese refer to the mindset as Mushin (a shortened version of the phrase mushin no shin loosely translating to mind without mind). This can be achieved when practicing a martial art technique, dancing, or doing repetitive movements. By being fully present in the physical movement, it allows us to get lost in the moment. This is the very nature of meditation.

Being in a flow state can open us to a new level of mental creativity. Flow also offers great opportunity to ponder questions and ideas that allow further introspection and problem-solving. This is another reason why we get some our best ideas when drifting off to sleep or standing in the shower. These states allow our mind and body the time to relax and therefore ponder deeper things.

From ten minutes of seated meditation to movement in flow states, these all help us get in front of the inevitable mental and physical slump, therefore allowing better performance in all that we do in the long run.

"Confine yourself to the present moment."

-Marcus Aurelius-

We don't remember days, we remember moments. You may not be able to remember what you did last weekend, yet you'll never forget your first kiss. Learn to enjoy the present moment, this one.

Yes, this moment right now.

Enjoy this moment, because your life is simply a collection of individual moments, just like this one, and each one is both precious and fleeting.

Even if the present isn't that appealing, understand the contrast it provides to appreciate the times that you genuinely enjoy. Whether this moment is agony or ecstasy, realize that it shall pass. Use this foresight to help you either endure or embrace whatever your moment holds.

Yes, this one.

I view myself as a teacher first and foremost. To be the best teacher possible means that I am ever the student. This humility keeps me open to learning and being lead into new areas of understanding. While these areas are often challenging, they are what cause the most growth. Even though I try to be the best teacher that I can be, I am far from the best. In fact, the best teachers aren't even people. By now you are familiar with your best teachers, they are already within you. Your pain and discomfort are your best teachers.

We remember painful lessons more than pleasurable ones because pain is a sensation designed to help us survive. From touching a hot stove to forgetting your coat when it's freezing outside, these times of discomfort at the lessons that stay with us the longest. These are the lessons that keep us alive.

You can tell how dearly someone's paid for a lesson in life by the amount of enthusiasm with which they teach that lesson. A person who has been through a terrible trauma will likely teach the lesson learned from it with exceptional detail, passion, and vigor, which explains why I've invested so much time, effort and emotion in writing this book.

The "A" Word

"You are stronger than you know or even realize, believe it."

-Marcus Aurelius Anderson-

There are many steps when it comes to being successful at anything in life. The first step begins with the correct mindset. This mindset is what is needed to create the idea and vision to be carried out. The second step is to act on the plan born from that vision. But there is the third component that everyone knows exists, but few want to acknowledge. Many are afraid that even mentioning this "elephant in the room" will cause it to crush them. What's the word that strikes fear into the hearts of those who like the "idea" of being successful but would rather be "busy" than genuinely productive? Accountability.

That's right, I said it. And we all know it's true. Even as I typed the word it made me feel uneasy, don't feel bad if it does the same for you. There are many people who will never even attempt the first step of success which is simply learning the correct mindset. Of those that have the mindset, even fewer can take the second step, implementation of the plan born from the proper mindset.

The reason people can be given the most prolific, life-changing information, yet still not act on it, is simple: They lack consequences, they lack accountability. Where there are no consequences, there are no results. Only when you know accountability, will you know results. In life, the repercussion of consequences is occurring all the time, but we are often unaware of them until they are already upon us. Even though accountability is inevitably approaching, it's happening too slowly to create urgency. Like a slow-sailing ship on the horizon, it seems too far off to be concerned about at the moment.

Eventually, people will come to a point when they do want to change. They get to this point when the pain of staying the same is greater than the pain of changing their current situation. At this point, they are willing to do whatever is necessary to become what they still have the potential to be. The question is, will they decide in time? Remember that even the correct decision becomes incorrect when acted on too late. This hesitation lets other things (aka "life") get in the way and impede their potential. This inevitably leads to compromise and distraction, which I've referred to in previous chapters. In other words, we make excuses, and an excuse is merely a premeditated lie.

Sickness, mental, and physical fatigue, as well as burn out, are all forms of Adversity, which is the ultimate form of accountability. Adversity is the ultimate form of accountability because it doesn't let up until you accomplish what is necessary to progress beyond it. It keeps presenting itself until you learn the lesson it's trying to teach you.

There will always be some form of Adversity in life, some days more so than others. Living with the urgency and knowledge that you may not always have the chance to work on the things that matter most to you keeps us accountable as well. Therefore, it's imperative to attack these tasks with all your energy. You must intellectually sprint towards your goals if you want them to become a reality. This sprint mentality is what makes you work as hard as possible to achieve your objectives. Knowing that you will only be working as hard as you can for a limited amount of time creates the urgency and accountability necessary to achieve more things with less time and effort. The 50 minutes of work to 10 minutes of rest protocol comes to mine.

What Did You Want to be?

There's a scene in the movie "Fight Club" when a store clerk is taken outside at gunpoint by Brad Pitt's character Tyler Durden. The clerk, named Raymond K. Hessel according to the identification in his wallet, is asked "What did you wanna be, Raymond K. Hessel?" to which he answers: "a veterinarian." Durden then asks why he quit school. Raymond responds that it was just too much school to take to become a vet. Durden pushes the gun barrel to Raymond's head asking him, "Would you rather be dead? Would you rather die? Here, on your knees in the back of a convenience store?!"

Tyler keeps Raymond's driver's license and says that if he doesn't follow through with his aspirations to become a veterinarian in the next six weeks, that he will come back and kill him. Raymond is set free and runs for his life. Adversity offers you no other choice and when there's no other choice, then the choice is simple. At that moment, Tyler Durden was Raymond's accountability; he was Adversity. Raymond truly believed that if he didn't do everything in his power to get into veterinarian school that this crazy psycho Tyler Durden would track him down and kill him. Tyler Durden's action (in the form of accountability) gave Raymond's life purpose and meaning.

Tyler Durden later says, "Tomorrow will be the most beautiful day of Raymond K. Hessel's life. His breakfast will taste better than any meal you and I have ever tasted."

My gift of Adversity had the same effect on me as the gun-wielding Tyler Durden did for Raymond K. Hessel. It gave me the true urgency to find purpose as well as act on it.

Accountability is something that cannot be overstated. The reason a person finds success with a personal trainer lies in accountability. If a personal trainer just emailed you a diet and workout routine and said, "Follow this diet and workout program and call me in 12 weeks", you'd be left to your own devices when you needed accountability the most. This means that you would likely lack the discipline needed to follow the diet closely and maintain the intensity and frequency of your workouts. However, if the trainer is banging on your door at 5 am and dragging your sorry ass out of bed and to the gym, that's another story. Knowing that the trainer will also be holding your accountable by putting you on a scale and measuring body fat levels every week would also be something that makes you put the donuts down and start eating healthier.

If that's not enough motivation, we can take it a step further. Imagine the trainer took a picture of you in a bathing suit. You are told that in three months they will take an "after" picture. Both the "before" and "after" picture will be posted on all social media platforms with all your friends and family to see. This represents a strong form of embarrassing "social accountability."

Let's be honest, if you're self-motivated to work out, there is a wealth of information at your fingertips regarding training routines, philosophies, and protocols. The same goes for diets. How many diets mention the same basic things? Lean meats, yep. Complex carbs, got it. Plenty of veggies, uh huh. You aren't telling me anything new. But, if you purchase a diet and workout program from a coach that you respect that will also implement "social accountability", it has much more gravity. The monetary investment is there because you respect this person enough to pay money to learn from them while the embarrassment factor cannot go overlooked. In fact, research indicates that paying for something makes a person 3x as likely to succeed than if they didn't pay for it. The reality is that, for better or worse, people don't respect what they don't pay for in one way or another. If they don't have to pay for something in some capacity, to them there is no value. They haven't had to hand over their hard-earned money for it, therefore in their mind, "it must not be worth much if it's free." People will pay money for a program that gets results. That's the whole reason they are willing to pay the price because all the guesswork has been taken out of it. They are paying for a plan that is successful and specific. Having some grand generalities isn't what they seek, they need concrete details that they can reproduce for themselves.

Having said that, people still don't like the idea of accountability because it means that there is another person who will be essentially judging their actions. The idea of this, in and of itself, is unappealing. Realize that by having someone keeping you accountable will not always mean that you will discuss successes. In fact, many times you will come to realize that you aren't progressing as far or as fast as you'd like.

No matter. What matters is the continued, consistent effort to improve. Keeping track of your progress is one of the best forms of accountability. Honestly reflecting on how much of your true potential you are reaching is the key.

For example, if you are making $150,000 a year while everyone around you is making $80,000 it may sound great. But you must still be honest with yourself. If your true potential is to make a $1,500,000 a year, then you are barely making 10% of what you're capable.

That's what accountability does, it keeps you honest and on the straight and narrow. It helps you get closer to you full potential, not just what you're comfortable achieving with minimal effort.

Accountability is one of the reasons I get the results that I do with my coaching clients. Having me as their coach makes them culpable for following through with the plan we have devised together. Anything in life worth having comes with a price.

Adversity is the price you must pay for greatness.

Information without accountability is just noise. Without accountability, even the most useful information is worthless. There are some great people out there who provide a ton of free information. A few have even gone so far as to say they aren't afraid of giving away this valuable information. Why? They say this because they know that 99% who hear the information won't act on it, while the other 1% are already implementing the information they are talking about.

While they may be giving some answers, what they aren't doing is giving the right questions. It's like being given the answer key to a test; while you have the answers, this information is still of little use without knowing the questions they correspond to.

Learning to ask the right question is often more important than answering a question that isn't at all relevant to your desired outcome.

There is something else that they aren't providing: Accountability. That lack of accountability, that free price, is what keeps people from acting and following through entirely. They are giving all the information but none of the context and none of the accountability. And that's what people need. The information is free; it's the accountability that costs you.

My injury made me take nothing for granted. The adage, "you don't know what you've got until it's gone" holds tremendous merit. The reality is that we DO know we've got, but we just never thought we'd lose it. Any talent, skill or gift you had before and get even a small amount of back becomes that much more precious. Instead of being bitter about the things I can no longer do, I am instead grateful for the ones that I can. This also makes me want to better refine the things of which I am capable, helping me savor and appreciate them all the more.

It's helped me not overlook the little things I now realize I'd taken for granted. Before when I would eat something delicious, I would taste the first few bites and then I would eventually become taste blind because I was no longer focusing on the moment. I let myself become distracted by something else, be it thinking of a future task in my mind, the current conversation or my cell phone. I had taken the taste for granted. I was never present enough to enjoy each bite as if it were the first. Now when I eat my favorite food, I try to act as if every bite is the first bite. I now try to savor everything I do, as if tasting a fine wine for the first time. Now foods taste better, smells are more vivid, and laughter is sweeter. Even if you don't care for the rain or cold weather, you will smile and appreciate it more when you walk in it if you were unable to even walk before.

Taking Stock

My injury helped solidify all the lessons I'd learned previously giving them more gravity. For me, wisdom was easy to recognize, even at a young age; but wisdom can be difficult to put into practice, regardless of age. If I'd have followed just this knowledge my entire life, I'd always have the 'what if?' In the back of my mind.

It's amazing what a little actual Adversity can do. Being faced with legitimate hardship helped me realize instantly what was important and what was not. It also helped me understand what I once thought was true and what was garbage. It's also helped me learn not to always take myself so seriously.

Chapter XI

Whitebelt

"Feelings assassinate the truth."

-Lacy French-

Getting My Ass Kicked

I met my Jeet Kune Do Sifu and dear friend LaDell Elliott 20+ years ago at an Aikido class he was observing. LaDell was very humble and approachable and we struck up a conversation about martial arts after class. The subject of Bruce Lee came up, and the conversation flowed from there. He later invited me to see his academy.

When I stepped into his school, I saw a Wing Chun Dummy, double end ball, and heavy bags. This was the same type of equipment I'd seen Bruce Lee training on in pictures. I was very impressed. LaDell asked if I'd like to spar, and I obliged. I had nearly ten years of Martial Arts experience between Aikido, Karate, and Tae Kwon Do at this point, so I felt that I could at least defend myself against most people. I learned quickly that LaDell Elliott was not like most people, not in the least.

The round started and from his southpaw stance, he immediately threw his right jab. It felt like I'd been hit with a sledgehammer. Next, he threw his lead hook kick so quickly; I barely had time to realize I'd been hit before the jab snapped out again, flowing seamlessly into a backfist. I tried to return with kicks and punches of my own but to no avail. I literally couldn't lay a glove on him. His footwork and head movement were like nothing I'd ever encountered. I felt like an antagonist in a Bruce Lee movie, and we all know what happened to those characters.

The entire time he was toying with me, he was nice about it. He could've caved my head in at any moment if he wanted to. Instead, he gave me a chance to try to work my technique, even though it was of little use. Afterwards, I had time to let the ass kicking I'd just received sink in.

The truth is sometimes ugly and brutal, especially when it slays a beautiful lie that we love to believe in. Even in that, truth is also lovely and kind. If you understand the nature of truth, you will never be led astray or blindsided. If you are, it was only because your knowledge of the truth was incomplete, unevolved, or you were simply not being honest with yourself by willfully believing in an illusion.

There are few things as devastating as having a romanticized ideology crushed by the weight of unflinching reality. I'd just been completely shut down by this guy; it was as if my prior years of training were useless. At this point, I had to be very honest with myself.

I could act like this humiliating event had never happened, the intellectual equivalent of putting my fingers in my ears and yelling "LA, LA, LA I CAN'T HEAR YOU!" or I could swallow my pride and acknowledge that I still had a tremendous amount to learn.

I was left with a choice.

I had a difficult decision to make. Technically, it was an easy decision, but my EGO made it difficult to let go. It was obvious which path I should take, but I had to muster the humility to empty my cup and start over as a rank beginner. Sometimes in life, we empty our cup willingly, sometimes someone else empties it for us. Being forced to question everything I knew to be true was causing so much cognitive dissonance it was overwhelming. What would I decide, the comfort of a fallacy or the discomfort of reality?

Finally, I let all these feelings go. I humbly ask LaDell how much lessons were and if he'd let me train with him. He happily agreed, and we've been great friends ever since.

Looking back on it now, I realize that I made the correct decision rather quickly compared to some people I've encountered in a similar situation. I could do this because my desire for useful knowledge was stronger than my desire to preserve my pride. In fact, I have found many who've experienced similar cognitive dissonance in other aspects of life who have willingly embraced the path of denial. To truly learn, we must be more willing to change our thinking than to convince ourselves that we are "right."

Why? Because it's much more comfortable to live in denial than to acknowledge the truth, and people do it every day. Many hunger for the truth, but the taste can sometimes be difficult to stomach.

> *"Do not seek the truth, only cease to cherish your opinions."*
>
> *-Zen Proverb-*

In my lifetime, I've started over in nearly a dozen martial arts, some simultaneously. And in every new art, none of my prior rank or experience was transferred to my belt ranking. In other words, even though I have a black belt or instructor level in other systems, I started all over again as a white belt. I had to empty my cup each time. While my experience of being an instructor and coach may help me learn perhaps a little faster than a student with no prior training, I must still give up the comfort and familiarity of rank to genuinely learn this new information.

I enter these unfamiliar realms seeking new experiences and information, which means I'm actively seeking discomfort.

Some may equate negativity with not being good at something right off the bat as if they can just jump into whatever new, bad ass endeavor they want and automatically become amazing at it without effort.

Think about that mentality for a second.

If whatever you wanted to try was easy, would you want to do it? What would be the incentive? Chances are the very thing that attracted you to this new challenging activity in the first place was the element of difficulty, excitement, or perceived danger associated with it. You likely want to learn this new knowledge because it's a skill that others don't readily possess.

How can you expect to learn from new experiences if you aren't willing to feel uncomfortable? How can you learn anything new if you aren't willing to try anything new!? Frankly, I enjoy starting over. I like the notion of a clean slate and the idea of learning something new for many reasons.

For one, it removes the pressure and allows me to focus on simply learning. I realize that my goal is to learn a new skillset and I'm not preoccupied with learning to defeat an opponent. In doing so, this also keeps me from taking myself too seriously. This reinforces the spirit of humility and makes learning that much easier.

Learning something new also gives me permission to fail in the process. In fact, I'm guaranteed to fail to some degree. I'm not supposed to be good at this new movement or technique because I'm a beginner. There are no desires, no expectations, only the experience of learning for learning's sake.

Stop Reinventing the Wheel

In my early teens, I fell in love with Stoicism, Taoism, and Zen. I devoured the writings of Marcus Aurelius, Lao Tzu, and Suzuki. These philosophies resonated with me. Even with this wisdom bestowed upon me, I still didn't heed all of it entirely.

While I recognized the wisdom within it, I still had the youthful exuberance that caused me to squander some of this knowledge. Luckily because of what I'd learned from these philosophies, I avoided many of the common pitfalls and dangers of adolescence growing up. However, I didn't always follow this higher thinking. And now that I'm older, I'm glad I didn't.

Had I followed just this knowledge my entire life, there would always be a part of me that would question and wonder. I would always have a 'what if?' in the back of my mind.

What if I went against these ancient tenets, what sort of repercussions would there be?

What if these writings only applied to the specific times and regions in which they were written?

What if all this stuff I was reading was flowery doublespeak and just plain wrong?

What if it was all bullshit?

While knowledge might be recognizable when read in a book, wisdom is harder to appreciate and put into practice, regardless of age.

It is said that youth is wasted on the young, but that's the nature of learning. Without the moments of misspent youth causing me to veer from "the path," there is no way of knowing if all the advice I'd been reading about was even worth the paper it was written on.

Youth has time on its side but lacks wisdom, while personal wisdom can only be learned through mistakes and experiences. These experiences require time, and we perceive to possess the most time in our youth.

The truth is anyone can repeat wise words, but to comprehend wisdom takes life experience. Understanding from experience is far greater than echoed insights and knowledge that's been well earned always holds the most value.

Knowledge is the collection of truths- wisdom is being able to apply them. I don't claim to have all the answers. Frankly, I know very little. What I do have are unique life experiences, and sharing them can help you find some of the answers you seek.

After all my adventures thus far in life, I'm glad that I've come full circle. The ancient lessons that I read and learned about 30+ years ago have had time to be repeatedly tested. This knowledge has now matured into wisdom, and I see more truth in these ancient lessons every day.

"Every musician is a thief and a magpie."

-Elvis Costello-

It's been said that if you steal from one author, it's plagiarism. If you steal from many, it's magically deemed "research."

226

The idea of being completely original is, in and of itself, completely unoriginal. Therefore, nothing that I write in this book can be original.

Nevertheless, for as long as I could remember, I'd tried to come up with something genuinely original to say. I wanted to create something unique that's never been heard before. I'd sometimes ponder this for hours. When I would come up with something that I thought was new and inventive, eventually I would read the same idea or sentiment in someone else's writings.

I even went through a snobbish phase of judging the writings and teaching of others thinking, "That's not original, that's the same thing 'so and so' said" or "that's exactly what they do in 'this or that' philosophy." I realize in hindsight I was doing this to justify my perceived lack of originality in thought, to make myself feel better. A form of intellectual sour grapes if you will.

Still, these shortcomings left me feeling deflated. I went through this process over and over so often that I almost wanted to give up.

Eventually, I had a breakthrough and was incredibly relieved. I no longer felt the weight of trying to make something unique, because frankly, it's just not possible.

I realized the reason I couldn't come up with anything new to contribute was because, as human beings, there's nothing I'm feeling, thinking, or experiencing that hasn't been felt by people from all walks of life over the centuries.

I laughed at myself for my self-centeredness.

Did I think that there is any emotion, feeling, or thought that I'd had as a human being that hasn't already been felt by millions of others for thousands of years before me? The hopes and dreams that people had during the height of the

Roman Empire are not different than ours today. Are we the first in existence to feel happiness, fear, fatigue, loneliness, ambition, love, or hate? Of course not.

The same is true for wisdom. There are no new lessons to be learned, only new ways to hear and apply them. There is nothing new under the sun, just more iterations of these truths; because truth stands the test of time. Every writer is a mockingbird and a thief. Every leader has their own way of saying something that's been said by countless others before. Many of the books on the bestseller list today are interpretations of a previous bestselling book from years before.

The reality is that all knowledge ultimately comes from the same source, it is just the name of the philosophy and region that it originates from that is different.

It's entirely possible that I may not teach you anything new. Perhaps I'll provide examples of how to combine some of these principles and ideas into something unique to you. Maybe I'll show you how to look at even the simplest things in a way that will make them new and even more valuable than you'd previously imagined.

To some, I may teach things they never knew about themselves. To others, I won't teach them anything new at all; I will teach them something even more important; I will remind them of things they have forgotten about themselves or truths that they have lost sight of.

You must remember that just because you've heard an idea or principle previously doesn't mean you should simply ignore it by thinking, "Yeah, yeah, yeah, I've heard that before." If you've heard it repeated often enough, you should realize a few things:

It should reinforce that this is indeed a worthy piece of advice. Think of it this way, what are the odds of history's greatest thinkers, leaders, and innovators coming to the same conclusions by accident? Initially, I'd become elated when I'd come up with something that was revolutionary to me. Alas, I'd become dejected when I'd read about someone else talking about the same idea or concept. Eventually, I realized that I should've been even happier! I'd come to the same conclusion by my own logic as some of the greatest intellectuals and philosophers in history! It would be like Lao Tzu or Epictetus coming up to me and saying, "I came to the same conclusion and completely agree with you!" How could I not be happy with that?! It means you should be following that repeated piece of advice even more than what you are currently to get the most from your efforts. If you've heard countless people that you respect continually mention that multitasking is worthless, but you continue to surf social media, while having a conversation on the phone the entire time you are working on a third, unrelated project on your laptop, you clearly haven't heard the lesson enough to take it to heart. If you hear the same piece of advice circulated by the best in the business, it's not the advice that is wrong; it's you. More to the point, it's your application of said information that's flawed. Your execution is what needs work. You must honestly redouble your efforts in implementing this often-repeated advice with greater attention to detail, then examine your results. You'll come to find your results will improve proportionally to the amount of genuine effort you put forth.

It should embolden you to realize that there is not much more needed for you to learn to achieve greatness. Many never start a project, business, or conversation because they think they must know more than what they do currently to begin. They think that they must know every possible step of the way to reach their destination. Here's the best advice I can give you: Stop trying to reinvent the wheel. If all the greatest minds throughout the centuries keep saying the same thing repeatedly, then you can save your energy and stop chasing your tail. This will keep you from constantly wondering if you're on the right path while letting you focus on the things that are more important such as commitment of execution.

With all that said, while I may not say anything original, I will try to say it in a way that is original.

Original Imitation

"Good artists copy, great artists steal."

-Pablo Picasso

My father is a great guitar player. He played in multiple bands while in high school, even playing in bars though he was underage at the time. I remember as a boy being mesmerized as I listened to him play practically any song that came on the radio perfectly by ear.

On the guitar, chords are to music as words are to conversation. When I was 12, my father taught me three chords: G, C, and D. While there are 1000's of possible chords in music, these are three of the most commonly played on the guitar. In music theory, these three chords form a simple I, IV, V progression; but for me, they formed hours of endless entertainment and self-discovery. I'd play until my fingers bled, then play some more. Once he saw that I was serious about learning more, my father bought me a Mel Bay's guitar chord book and my musical vocabulary grew even more.

One fateful day, I saw the historical footage of Jimi Hendrix performing his interpretation of the National Anthem at Woodstock. My head nearly exploded. It was one of the most incredible things I'd ever witnessed in my young life. Hendrix's level of mastery was on full display as he and the guitar expressed their musical vision as one. He was completely lost in the passion of his performance, the raw emotion of the music he created was palpable. From that day forward, I tried to recreate that performance. I had no idea how I was going to do it, but I was determined to try. From this exercise of imitation, I learned many lessons.

The first lesson I learned was that there was only one Jimi Hendrix. The second lesson was that I sounded nothing like him whatsoever.

As a beginner, even if you try to imitate and copy another musician, author or artist, you simply don't have the technical skill set to look or sound like that person, but if properly motivated, you will repeatedly try to do so, and that's the secret.

On the journey of imitation, you'll make mistakes; and that's precisely how you'll learn.

You'll stumble upon other sounds that aren't what you are seeking, but you'll still like the discovery. This is how you begin to collect different tones and textures which will eventually be the beginnings of your own voice, style, and sound.

While I never sounded exactly like Hendrix, trying to sound like him led me to discover other musicians and styles that I fell in love with. I was hooked by Jimmy Page's undeniable riffs in Led Zeppelin. I was blown away by the speed and power of Eddie Van Halen's guitar solos. I became enamored with the classical guitar virtuosity of Segovia. In the beginning, I would set out to play each of these different styles separately, as if they were the curriculum of a specific class in school. On a whim, I began to combine these unique styles for fun. The sound was interesting, to say the least.

By attempting to imitate many different guitarists, I gained a larger musical vernacular. As I let these and other influences flow through me, the multitude of different sounds culminated into something I'd never heard before. I was then able to create something that was uniquely my own style, my own voice.

Originally, I was afraid to sound like somebody else be it writing or in music. I now realize that I couldn't do that even if I tried. I couldn't sound exactly like another author because my writing is always evolving as I learn.

Take "Meditations" by Marcus Aurelius for example. We must remember that his writings will never change because he cannot write anything more than what he has already written. But I am alive and constantly learning and evolving. No matter how much I try to make my writings sound like his timeless prose, mine will continue to sound different and unique because my experiences are different and unique to his. Your voice will sound different than mine and others because of your unique path.

This is path of discovery found in every art form- be it music, painting, writing, or any other creative process. We are moved by the emotion conjured by a song, watercolor or passage in a book. It is by such happenstance that we begin the journey of self-expression in our chosen medium.

"I am a finger pointing at the moon, don't look at me; look at the moon."

-Buddha-

While no thought may be truly original, it sounds original to the person hearing it for the first time.

While there were parts of the service industry that were sometimes less than desirable, I truly enjoyed my time working behind the bar. I learned a tremendous amount about human behavior and motivation while making lifelong friends in the process.

The vocation of bartender encompasses much more than just the ability to pour a good drink. There are many soft skills and other intangibles that make a person worthy of the bartender moniker. While tending bar I was everything from a motivator and big brother, to a shoulder to cry on and bouncer, sometimes all within moments of one another.

Being a "modern urban psychiatrist" was also a big part of the job description. Over time, patrons would inevitably come seeking advice about their troubles. I'd offer a solution based on what I'd read by many philosophers and intellectuals. They'd often be happy and impressed with the answer to which I'd say, "Don't be impressed with my answer, I'm just paraphrasing what a person much smarter to myself said and did." Many would respond, "I don't care if someone else said it because I've never heard it before and I'm just glad I have the answer, thank you!"

The lesson is that just because something is apparent to one doesn't mean that it's easily visible to another. To the person who's never heard something before, no matter how tired and old it may seem to one who knows, it is new. And there are plenty of answers that are elementary to some that would seem earth-shattering to others.

I'd also have a few who'd tell me, "I've heard that advice many times before, but somehow the way you said it just made it click!" In the business of advertising and sales, it is said that barring impulse buys, it takes anywhere from 5-12 exposures or contacts to get a sale. These exposures and contacts are in the form of a follow-up phone call or email. In advertising, it means that it takes 5-12 times hearing the advertisement on the radio or seeing it on T.V. Therefore, someone may have heard a principle that I've mentioned, but the way I told them may have been the equivalent of the 12th time they've heard it. That's when it resonates with them, creating that much sought after "A-HA!" moment of understanding.

Accept Truth Wherever You Find It

Looking back, I realize that there have been many times in my life when my learning has been compromised by my intellectual prejudices. Therefore, I urge you to accept truth wherever you can find it. More importantly, don't reject truth simply because it comes from a lesson or a person that you may not care for.

Don't shoot the messenger. I quote many people in this book. Some are quotes you know while others may be new to you, but to absorb the most useful information from these bits of knowledge, you should take them for what they are. This means you must not judge the source.

There are some grammatical errors in this book as I'm sure you've already noticed. I insisted that they remain in the final draft to make a point. If the gravity of my message and story is lessened because of a misspelled word or the semantics of pronouns, then obviously I haven't done my job. I trust that my voice and lessons aren't watered down by something as insignificant as a punctuation, and I hope that you are willing to accept the quality of truth I convey regardless of the smoothness of medium in which they are delivered. Please don't let a typo hinder your ability to appreciate the value of the message. The reality is that we can learn the most from even the most flawed people.

"Ask not what your country can do for you...ask what you can do for your country."

Many will recognize this infamous quote. It was stated by the 35th President of the United States John F. Kennedy in his inaugural address. John Kennedy was a historical

President for many reasons. Kennedy was the youngest elected United States President in history. He championed Civil Rights and was responsible for the Equal Pay act of 1963. JFK also established the Peace Core, lead the country out of recession, and averted nuclear war during the Cuban Missile Crisis.

"If you want to change the world, go home and love your family."

This is a quote attributed to Mother Teresa, whose legacy is undeniable. She founded a hospice called "The Home for the Dying" that allowed those with a terminal illness to pass away with dignity while being surrounded by compassion in 1952. Her years of tireless work was eventually recognized in 1979 when she was awarded the Nobel Peace Prize. In true Mother Teresa fashion, she refused the usual ceremony given to the award recipient and instead asked to have the $192,000 prize (equivalent to nearly $650,000 today when adjusted for inflation) given to the sick and poor in India.

"Struggle is the father of all things. It is not by the principles of humanity that man lives or preserves himself above the animal world, but solely by means of the most brutal struggle."

This often-overlooked quote was written by a person whose motivational speeches literally changed the lives of millions around the world. The reason most English speakers don't recognize the quote is that it was originally written in German...by Adolf Hitler. I beg of you dear reader, before you begin to write a venom soaked email, please hear me out. Yes, Adolf Hitler was clearly an evil monster of the highest degree and I am not defending or agreeing with him even in the slightest. His anti-Semitic beliefs and acts are responsible for the most notorious acts of genocide in modern history. He was absolutely a horrendous human being that is deserving of the hate his name evokes.

This is an example of how difficult it can be to accept truth irrespective of source. How do you know if what you're hearing is the truth if it is from somebody that you absolutely despise? Because it will probably anger you, and this is your indicator. It will anger you because you know that it is true.

When I read the quote initially, it made sense to me. But when I found out who wrote it, I was utterly ashamed of myself. Realizing that I agreed with anything that this wicked creature had written made me feel sick to my stomach. So, does that mean that I should throw away the value found in these words? Should I not use his rise to power as a cautionary tale and an example of what not to do?

While John F. Kennedy was an incredible President, his extramarital affairs and indiscretions were a thing of legend. Yet that does not take away from all the groundbreaking things he did for the United States.

While Mother Teresa achieved sainthood, it has been documented that nearly the last half-century of her life had been lived literally in a crisis of faith. Yet this doesn't lessen the positive impact she made on thousands of impoverished lives with her life's work.

Almost like cutting the bruised part off a banana, realize that it's entirely possible to intellectually extract the knowledge regardless of source, and use it for good. The truth is unchanging, but our understanding of it is ever evolving. Truth takes no sides and has no preferences; it simply exists without political affiliation or motives. To learn as much as we can, we should view truth in the same unbiased manner. Only then can we begin to apply it to change the world.

Chapter XII

Recap

"I cannot teach anybody anything, I can only make them think."

-Socrates-

This book was originally going to be broken down into three different books with each covering different aspects of my mindset, recovery, action steps, and examples.

Ultimately, I decided to condense the most important aspects of each section to create a single, easily readable book. This lets me provide substance by drawing on my own stories and experiences to create greater quality and depth of content for the reader.

Today, though I still have permanent nerve damage, I'm able to walk and use my hands while living an amazing life. I would never be able to do the things I've done to help empower others without the Gift of Adversity. I live with pain and numbness in my hands and feet, and for that I am grateful.

I am grateful because this pain reminds me of how far I've come and that compared to where I was when I was injured, I'll gladly take some discomfort. As I've mentioned time and again, Adversity truly is relative.

Concepts > Specifics

People may forget specific details about a book, but they can usually tell you the basic concepts. They can then tell you how said concepts impacted them and made them feel.

You won't remember all the intricacies of a complicated multi-step plan. However, if you understand the concept, you can create any plan necessary to achieve your desired goal. Instead of accentuating the semantics and differences in something, try to see the overarching truths.

My intent is to provide timeless examples of principles and concepts that can be applied to everything from business and leadership to personal development and relationships. By understanding a principle, you start to understand the essence of multiple other subjects more quickly. You will also begin to see many similarities in seemingly unrelated subjects that were previously invisible.

It is my hope that the reader can come back to this book on multiple occasions, finding something new or overlooked from the previous reading each time. I would be honored if this book became one that the reader would recommend or give as a gift to others needing these lessons and wisdom.

The things discussed are universal. My goal is to help you discover your own truth, whatever that truth may be, and then continue to learn more from it for as long as you so desire.

What's the lesson?

In this life there are no sides, no enemies, only teachers.

Remember that at any time, in any situation, you can always ask yourself the following question:

"What can I glean that's valuable from this person or this situation?"

This is the question I've been forced to ask myself time and again in many areas of my life. And while posing the question is easy, applying it honestly to ourselves and our situation is likely one of the most difficult things you'll ever do.

The answers that we desire most are always guarded by Adversity, but these are the only answers worth seeking.

Once you understand this concept, you'll start seeking it out. You'll begin to actually crave Adversity.

It is at that point that you can see your Adversity for what it is, as an indicator of opportunity. It's a chance to learn, to grow stronger, and learn more about ourselves.

The greater the Adversity, the greater the potential reward. In this way, Adversity is tremendous a gift.

It's important to keep this in mind as we are battling Adversity, because it is in the moment that we most want to quit that we must fight the hardest.

Remember that Adversity doesn't want to give up the gift it protects.

Adversity is a gift, embrace it.

Gratitudes

First and foremost, I'd like to thank you the reader. It is for you that this book was written. I hope my story helps you through whatever Adversity that you are currently facing. You are stronger than you even know, believe that.

I'd like to thank my mother for all her love and support. I can't imagine my life without her, she's my favorite woman in the world.

I love my father more than life itself, he is the man who taught me the importance of work ethic and character. He and my Great Uncle are the reason I am the man I am today.

My Great Uncle and my father were the two best role models a young man could ever ask for. I wish my Great Uncle was alive to see this book published.

I'd also like to express my love and gratitude to the rest of my family and dear friends, you've influenced me more than you even know.

I want to thank LaDell Elliott and all my extended martial arts family around the world. The people that I have had the pleasure of meeting through the martial arts since I was a child until now has helped forge the mentality that made me strong enough to overcome Adversity.

Buddy Jacobucci was by my side through the entire time of my injury, I cannot thank him enough for his help and friendship. Thanks man.

Basil Reid is a great man, warrior and scholar. I treasure our friendship to this day, he's taught me lessons that I'm still trying to grasp and fully understand. Thanks Baz.

Lastly, I'd like to thank every hardship I've ever encountered, it is these Adversities that forced me to see the gift they present.

Acknowledgements

No man is an island. Much in the same way it takes a village to raise a child, it takes a team to create, shape and launch a successful book. The following people have been instrumental in this process regarding "The Gift of Adversity." Without their undying dedication, the book would never have seen the light of day.

Lacy French is not only an incredibly talented editor, graphic designer, and creative ninja— she's also a dear friend. She has built an amazing website and created multiple graphic design projects for me in addition to editing this book. She believed in and supported me well before my TEDx talk "The Gift of Adversity." I simply cannot thank her enough. www.greymatterdesign.co

I'd like to thank Photographic Designs by Rachel Williams. Rachel Williams did a truly phenomenal job capturing my image in a way that is a very real representation of me. Rachel also did an incredible job designing the book cover as well as the exceptional portrait photography. www.pdgallery.net

I'm incredibly grateful and thankful to Keith Politte and his tremendous TEDx CoMo 2017 crew. It was Keith's willingness to grant me a TEDx stage that's lead to endless possibilities. I'm so honored to have shared the stage with all the talented TEDx speakers at the event in Columbia Missouri.

I'd also like to thank the following people for giving me the opportunity to come on their show and talk about my story and book. I'm honored and humbled that they felt me worthy of such an opportunity.

-Greg Swanson's "Warrior Mind" podcast.

-Bob Choat's "School of Transformation" podcast.

-Sean DeLaney's "What Got You There with Sean DeLaney" podcast.

-Calin Saft's "Men's Journey Today" podcast.

-Rafa Conde's "Man of War: Forging Men into Warriors" podcast.

-Tommy Malone's "Blending the Family" podcast

-Laura Coe's "The Art of Authenticity" podcast

-Jerry Gaura's "Pioneers of Insight" podcast

-Chris Cebollero's "The Ultimate Leadership" podcast

-Ron Malhotra's "The Successful Male" podcast

-MAX NOBLE's premier episode of the first LinkedIn video talk show in history "Share Your Wisdom."

-Robert Orion Sikes' "Keto Savage" podcast

I'd also like to thank Christi Morgan for helping me better understand social media and use it to create a bigger positive impact.

Last but not least, I'd like to give a big thank you to all of my fans and connections on social media for their support.

Made in the USA
Coppell, TX
13 July 2021

58914196R00138